A PATCHWORK FAMILY

A PATCHWORK FAMILY

Mark and Mary Frances Henry

Foreword by Lyman Coleman

BROADMAN PRESS
Nashville, Tennessee

DEDICATION

Dedicated to our family,
both natural and extended.

ACKNOWLEDGMENTS

Our book is about learning and being and growing and living. It grows out of experiences with special people. Our extended family group has given of itself, reading and contributing and allowing us to share special times. With much love and gratitude to:

George and Barbara Brightwell
Judy Bulay
Burley and Frances Burleson
Ron Hall
Johnny King
Tom and Marsha Lawson and Tim and Judy
Cathy Quinlan
Sylvia Richards
and to our own children—Mike, Matt, and Mende
Henry

As we started planning the book, Hal and Wanda Johnson gave valuable insights and ideas and let us bounce ideas around with them. Their help in both educational theory and theological interpretation was essential.

Dick Waggener gave frequent and valuable feedback, and his insights into family growth have been most helpful.

Clear Lake Presbyterian Church was the testing ground for many of our ideas and designs, as well as providing a church home in which people can grow.

Anne Wallace and Laura Kelley typed, corrected, and read the manuscript, and we thank them both.

Wally and Esther Howard convinced us originally that we had a story to tell. Without that encouragement, we might not have started.

And a special thank you to our friend, Jim Simmons who, through his personal faith, started us on a journey that led to this ministry.

ABOUT THE COVER PHOTO

Our "family" quilt. Each square was prepared by a family member as a statement of his or her growing edge of faith. The tree in the center is the tree of life. The roots with the eighteen hearts symbolize the love that supports our family life. From Ephesians 3, "I pray that you may have your roots and foundation in love, so that you, together with all God's people, may have the power to understand how broad and long, how high and deep, is Christ's love." The thirty-six leaves in the branches are a statement of the multiplying power of that love. The Christian symbols bring us together in Christ. Again from Ephesians 3, " . . . the Father, from whom every family in heaven and on earth receives its true name."

PHOTO CREDITS: *Cover*—Elder Larson, Houston Texas
Inside Photos of "Family"—Ron Hall and George Brightwell, both of Houston, and members of the "Family"
Photos of Mark, Mary Frances, and their children—Gary Walston, Springfield, Virginia

PERMISSIONS

All quotations from *Why Am I Afraid to Tell You Who I Am?* are reprinted from *Why Am I Afraid to Tell You Who I Am?* by John Powell © 1969 Argus Communications. Used with permission from Argus Communications, Niles, Illinois.

The quotation from *Beyond Ourselves* is from *Beyond Ourselves* by Catherine Marshall. Copyright 1961 McGraw-Hill Book Company. Used by permission of McGraw-Hill Book Company.

All resources and quotations from Lyman Coleman are used by his permission.

"Eight Principles of Covenant Groups" (in Chapter 9) is reprinted from *Faith at Work* magazine, October, 1975. Used by permission of Word, Inc.

"The Care and Feeding of IALACS" by Esther Howard (in Chapter 13) is reprinted from *Faith at Work*, March, 1974. Used by permission of Word, Inc.

Word, Inc., has granted permission for all other quotes and references from *Faith at Work magazine*.

Material from *Come to the Party* by Karl Olsson is used by permission of Word Books © Copyright • 1972.

Material from *The Family Together, Intergenerational Education in the Church School* by Jack and Sherry Rogers is used with permission of Acton House © Copyright • 1976.

Material concerning the Johari Window, including the illustration on page 100, is reprinted from *Group Processes: An Introduction to Group Dynamics* by Joseph Luft, by permission of Mayfield Publishing Company © 1970 by Joseph Luft.

The quotation from "The Wedding Banquet" by Sr. Miriam Therese Winter is © MCMLXV by Medical Mission Sisters, Philadelphia, Pa. Reprinted by permission of Vanguard Music Corp., 250 W. 57th St., N. Y., N. Y.

Rev. Claxton Monro and Ms. Bonnie Agar have given permission to quote them.

A RHYTHM STORY: THE PRODIGAL SON by Rev. Gordon Nyenhuis is used with the permission of Mr. Nyenhuis.

The Scripture reference marked TEV is from the *Today's English Version of the New Testament*. Copyright American Bible Society 1966.

FOREWORD

Mark and Mary Frances Henry! You are to be commended! You have done what many of us have been asking for—you have put together a practical guide for family groups in the church, with just enough theory and know-how to get us started.

And the blow-by-blow account of your own family group makes the theory come alive. (I still can't believe you told the story about your own little girl: "Daddy, I gotta go now").

I hope *A Patchwork Family* is read by every pastor, every church leader, every parent in the church. I hope this story gets through to concerned Christians who are struggling to build better family relationships in a society that seems to tear the family apart.

Yes, and I hope this book is taken seriously by the church leaders who are responsible for planning church activities . . . that split up the family.

From my own observation in scores of churches, however, there seems to be little statistical difference between family crises among those related to the church and those outside the church.

The church, in other words, often seems to be doing very little to bring families together or build better family relationships. In fact, the present approach of splitting up the family in our church programs may be a contributing factor to the problem—not the solution.

This is the reason why I find Mark and Mary Frances' book on family groups so exciting. They have given us a workable plan for bringing the family together—and enough practical suggestions for running family groups in the church for months.

Now, with *A Patchwork Family*, we have another way of accomplishing the task—and all kinds of suggestions to help us in strengthening programs in the church.

Mark and Mary Frances, thank you for giving us your gifts—and a dream for the future.

Lyman Coleman
Serendipity House

INTRODUCTION

This is a book for you to use. It is born out of our experience, mostly joyous, occasionally painful, but always growth producing. It is incomplete. It is still in process, still being written. Through it we hope to share with you ideas, methods, and a touch of theory so that you can find growth and fun also. We are still growing, and we hope that process never stops.

The book is also our answer to a personal need for a how-to-do it book on intergenerational small groups. When we first tried this approach to family growth several years ago, we could find no books or resource material that would tell us what to do. So we created our own, and we offer it to others who are searching for a way to grow as a family.

For several years we have been in, led and worked with small groups, both in our own church and through Faith at Work. As this became an ever growing personal ministry, we found demands on our family time increasing. That created a real problem within our family. In our zeal to help save the world, we were losing touch with our own children. Can you think of a more serious error than trying to save the world and, in the process, losing your own children? Somehow, we had to regain that important balance that would provide time for each other and for them. It was not an easy problem to solve.

As we talked and prayed for an answer, we kept coming back to one point. If the open, honest supportive life-style we were experiencing in small groups was really that valid, if it really is of God, then it should work for all ages. But everything we had learned about small-group dynamics said that children simply could not handle the group process, that they would become disinterested and disruptive. Several times we discarded the idea of including them, but we could find no other alternative.

We finally came back to it. Why not try a small group with children, adults, all ages? Yeah, why not all ages? Why not an intergenerational group, a family? After all, isn't that what small groups are all about? To be a family is to have someone we can depend on to share the joys and hurts of life with, to call when we need someone.

In his group work, Lyman Coleman uses the question, "If you needed someone at 3:00 A.M. for a real life or death situation, who would you call?" For all too many of us, the answer is "no one." Some might say the family. But what do you do if the family is several hundred or even several thousand miles away?

America is on the move today. We are a mobile society. The old family ties with our parents, grandparents, uncles, aunts, and cousins are rapidly disappearing with the years. Even the word family is taking on new meanings. Today's family can be two parents with children, a single parent with children, adults with no children or whose children are grown, or even a single adult. In addition, other forces in our society pull at the family. Even the service clubs—Scouts, garden club, etc., all of which are good and serve valuable purposes—have a tendency to draw the family apart. All of these clubs are for individuals within the family rather than for the family as a unit.

The church is the one place where we can counter this trend. But we are not doing it even in church! We split the family apart as soon as it comes through the front door of the church. We send the children to their Sunday School class, the adults to theirs. We even break the adults into the single's class, the men's class, the women's class, the over sixty-year-old class.

The church does provide a starting point, perhaps the only one left today. At least the family is together when it comes to church. How can we keep them together, and enable each person to communicate meaningfully with the others as persons? We believe the intergenerational small group is a way to answer this question. It has worked for us. We have seen it work for others. Sure, it takes work, commitment, and some sacrifice. But can you think of anything that is of value that doesn't take work and commitment and some sacrifice? And it is worth it. To see your children grow emotionally and relationally as well as physically; to feel growth within yourself; to be loved and accepted for who you are—that is grace, God's grace.

So we want to share with you how this has happened, and is happening in our lives. We believe it can happen for you.

Let us begin. As we said, the book is still in process, still being written. It is being written for those who want to extend a life-style—to care more and to be cared for. As you read, we invite you to share with us and become a part of the fun and excitement of being.

Mark and Mary Frances Henry and their immediate family

CONTENTS

To see your children grow emotionally and relationally, as well as physically; to feel growth within yourself; to be loved and accepted for who you are—that is grace, God's grace.

1

Who Are We? Who Are You?

In communicating with a person, we've found there is something helpful about knowing that person, or at least knowing something about who and what he values. It's far more fun, for example, to read a book if you know the person who wrote it. We wish there were some way we could meet and share with each of you individually, because we believe that would make the sharing process and the relationship building so much easier. Since that isn't very practical, we can at least let you know what assumptions we made in writing this book. We can let you know where we're coming from. Hopefully that will give us a good start in establishing a relationship with you.

OK to Disagree

First of all, we want you to feel OK about not agreeing with everything we say. Disagreement is normal, natural, and we expect it, as long as in disagreeing we can respect each other as persons. What we say in these pages comes from our experience, interpreted and evaluated through our understanding of Scripture and our own lives.

We would like to share with you some of the assumptions and values we accept. We want to work within the framework of the Christian faith. Recognizing that many interpretations exist for this term, we do not want to get **17** into a lengthy dialogue on the fine points of theology.

Jesus, the Living Son of God

Let us just say that we believe Jesus Christ is the living Son of God, that he is a real, live person with whom we can talk, share, play, hurt, and love. He is a man, and he is much more than a man. He is God in person. We can relate in a very human way with the man Jesus who lived with people, who walked the dusty roads and rough streets of cities and countryside. He is a man who could express his anger and love, who could feel rejection and hatred aimed at him, who suffered staggering pain on the cross. And he is the man who after three days of numbing death walked into the midst of his followers to give them and us his Father's grace, love, and forgiveness. He is our friend, our companion, our Lord, and Savior.

We also say that, from our own encounters with him, Jesus Christ is not an intellectual exercise; he is an experience. As we have worked with groups, especially those with younger children (and a young child can be chronologically aged six to one hundred), we have come to believe that a child experiences love, grace, and God long before he can intellectually understand the concepts these words stand for. Without that experience, the intellect cannot fully grasp the reality of God's love.

There are as many ways to experience God as there are people. Many of our experiences with God are through other people. If we can, through a group situation, better enable this type of experiential learning, the more intellectual and academic study later on will become more meaningful, hopefully easier, and more productive. We are in no way suggesting that Christian growth is purely emotional or experiential. The study of God's Word is vitally important and serves as a measure against which we check out our experiences. At the same time, the purely intellectual approach is not complete, and particularly with children is just not going to work. So we are focusing our attention on the experiential in this book. The bookstores and libraries are full of excellent studies in the theological and psychological arenas. Our desire is to share with you the experiences, fun, surprises, and joys of discovery that live within each one of us, you and me.

We will talk about the importance of play, of allowing the natural child within each of us to have time in the sun. We believe there is a significance in the connection between the "natural child" as defined in the world of Transactional Analysis (TA) and Jesus' words about coming to him as a child (Matt. 18:1–6). Can we really come to him when that natural child is repressed, kept from being? We don't think so.

Abundant Life—Relationships

We believe that the Christian life is a life of relationships; relationships that are honest, responsible, and caring. We cannot be Christians alone. Faith at Work in Columbia, Maryland, has for several years talked about the importance of four relationships in the Christian life. These are our relationships with God, with ourselves, with others, and with the world around us. If any of these are out of balance in our lives, the total is out of balance. One of our main thrusts in this book is to help you learn to design exercises and activities that will enable you to grow in these four areas of relationships. Some will focus on one particular relationship, others will aim at more than one. All exercises and activities will be fun and exciting because they are done with other people, and people are fun and exciting if we allow and expect them to be. We were recently visiting with Claxton Monro, rector at St.

Stephen's Episcopal Church in Houston, talking about intergenerational groups. He made a statement which has so much meaning to us. To quote him, "We are told that Jesus came into the world that we might have life more abundantly; not religion more abundantly, but life." Abundant life equals abundant relationships!

In our work we want to claim the words in Genesis about God creating man and then saying, "It is good." Now we know that we are sinners; there is no question that we are all sinners. The question is whether we can know that we are loved, accepted, and forgiven with the same certainty that we know we are sinners.

We believe grace is the key to living the Christian life abundantly. God's coming among us tells us that he accepts, forgives, and loves us, and that he considers us acceptable, forgivable, and lovable. The hard part is for us to claim this grace for ourselves. But who are we to question God? To say that we are totally worthless, totally unworthy, is perhaps to say that God does make some "junk." That just isn't consistent with what we hear the Scriptures saying.

Our experience is that the fully abundant life flows freely, joyfully, and spontaneously out of an awareness of grace. Because of God's grace, there is a goodness in each of us, a limitless potential waiting to be tapped, opened, enabled, and loved into reality. People usually become whatever is expected of them. For our groups, let's expect the best. Let's expect people to become who they are meant to be by their Creator. Let's expect people to care. Good relationships are caring relationships.

In no way do we want to deny the reality of our bad sides, but so much has been said about that already. Need we say more? Try something as you are reading. Would you check out your own life-style? Does your religion

20 result in bad feelings of guilt, worthlessness, and in general putting oneself down? Or, does it result in good feelings of being acceptable, capable, and loved by God? Are you claiming and living the grace that Christ brings to believers?

So we are emphasizing the position of affirming goodness and personhood, of enabling creation to continue in each of us as God means it to and really wants it to.

We have told you a little about who we are. Now, who are you? We can imagine that you may be a church professional, or you may be a struggling lay person trying to find a way to put some real meaning back into your family life and family communications. Or you may be somewhere in between the professional and the lay person. We have that in common with you as we struggle to find new life. By sharing our experiences we are relating to and with you, and out of sharing will come the validity for those of you to whom this book will be meaningful. You can expect openness and honesty in our words, as we share as accurately as we can what has happened to us. Our sharing will include growth in faith as we move toward the maturity that the Scriptures talk about. We are a long way from it, but we are on the road and hopefully making progress. We hope our words and thoughts will enable others to experience the joy and fun of growing in relationships, and also the healing power of relationships in the abundant life.

2

Small Groups, People's Needs, and Other Assorted Thoughts

This is a book about intergenerational groups in the church. Intergenerational is such an awesome word—big, impressive sounding. We keep looking for a less frightening word, but so far our culture hasn't offered one. Anyway, what exactly is an intergenerational group? We define it as a small group that includes at least three generations. Before going any further, though, we probably need to define small groups as *we* use the term. An intergenerational group is a type of small group, and we need some common understandings with you about how such groups work.

Renewed Interest in Small Groups

Recent years have seen a renewed interest in small groups in the church. It is not a new idea. Small groups have been a part of the Christian church from the beginning. Jesus and his twelve disciples were a small group. They shared their dreams, fears, joys, and hurts. They supported each other. Jesus needed their support, and they needed him.

After Jesus left them the eleven continued to meet, sharing their lives, preparing for Pentecost. They were not sure what was coming next, nor were they aware of the significance their small group would have on the future.

As the church began to develop after Pentecost, many of those first cells were small groups. The pattern continues through the history of the church. John Wesley and the Quakers used small groups for support and learning. And today we see a new interest in this ministry.

Secular groups have received a lot of attention recently. Sensitivity groups, T-groups, and therapy groups have become popular. So, it's not just in the church.

We believe that people invest their time and energy in things that meet their needs, or at least seem to. We all have needs, emotional and physical. We need the support of others. We need to feel loved and accepted. We need affirmation. We need to know that we are important to others, and that they care. We need the freedom to share our ideas, thoughts, and feelings. We need to be known and accepted for who we really are. Very often we hide ourselves emotionally from others, even our close friends. It's like wearing a mask. When we show our masked selves to others, we also hide from God. Yes, he knows it, and so do we. Yet we still play the game. Why?

John Powell gives a solid answer in his book, *Why Am I Afraid to Tell You Who I Am?* "Because if I tell you and you don't like me, that's all I have." The good news of Christ is that whatever we have is enough for him. But we need to experience that kind of acceptance from other people. So we look for it in small groups. And it happens. And when it happens, the results are life changing. WOW!

Why a Small Group?

Another question is significant. Why does it have to be a "small" group? Why only eight to twelve people? Why didn't Jesus get himself organized and go on big crusades in a caravan of hundreds or even thousands? Modern psychology has put into words what Jesus lived. Close, honest, trusting relationships are necessary to meet the needs we are talking about. To develop such relationships requires time, emotional energy, and a commitment to each other. We each have only a limited amount of this time and energy. We can handle only a few such relationships at a time. Jesus chose only twelve. As a human being, he experienced the same needs we do. He understood that to have the quality of relationship he needed, his support group had to remain small.

Vital Ministry

We see small groups as a vitally important ministry within the church today. People respond to the group experience in different ways. Most people experience joy and growth. A few may come away less enthusiastic. The chances of having a good experience become greater if we know how groups function.

A lot of good material is available today on group dynamics. A lot of it sounds very complicated, very psychological. It doesn't have to be complex. Lyman Coleman has described group process or group dynamics in a simple, easy to understand analogy. He has written a series called "Serendipity Books" that are good. If you aren't familiar with his work, go to the bookstore and invest in them. Then use them.

In his work, Lyman writes that a group will go through four phases in its lifetime. To illustrate this, he uses a baseball diamond. To reach first base, a group must do some history giving—sharing with each other who they are as individuals. To reach second base, he suggest they affirm each other, tell each other the good things they see. The TA folks call this "positive stroking." Jesus did a lot of it. He called forth Peter's strengths. He affirmed Mary Magdalene. And they trusted him. That happens in a group, and this trust is essential. With trust, the group moves on to third base, sharing dreams and goals, doubts and fears. Lyman calls this phase "goal setting." This is the point at which group members can begin to honestly raise questions of faith, to share special dreams and hopes, to even share the fears of life. From there, it's a short run to home plate—*koinonía*, the Greeks called it. A modern term would be a "family of Christ." This is the point at which a small group experience can approach the experiences of those first Christians. Lyman suggests discussion and sharing questions that will enable a group to move through these four phases. They are excellent, nonthreatening, and a lot of fun.

The beauty of Lyman's model is its simplicity. We haven't found anything better. In practice, groups will go through the phases differently. Some will go quickly, others more slowly. The phases will probably overlap. One of the fascinations of working with small groups is that each one is unique. Out of that uniqueness comes the answer to another question. After we reach home base, then what? The answer is within the group. The group decides, based on their own needs as a group. We'll say more later about some possibilities for the intergenerational group.

This is probably a good place to talk about what a small group *is not*. That's on the negative side, true, but there are some key points. Groups can be misused with negative results. By knowing a few of the possibilities, hopefully, we can avoid them.

First, a small group in the church is not a therapy group. It may be very therapeutic, but it is not a therapy group. Therapy groups are a tool for use only by trained professionals. Let's keep the difference clearly in mind. **25**

We want to grow, to share, to enjoy the relationships in the group. We do not want to try to psychoanalyze anyone.

Another concern often voiced by pastors is that *groups can become cliques*. That is a valid concern. It can happen. We believe that good leadership training will minimize this danger. From our experience, the rewards far overshadow the risks. Also, by integrating the small groups into the total life and ministry of the church, we avoid the group's becoming a "church within a church." When people's needs are met, they will reach out to others. The quality of the group relationship can enable this kind of outreach. When this happens, cliques and "churches within the church" are pretty unlikely.

Maintaining a discipline of prayer in each group meeting will keep our attention focused on Christ. Though discipline is a hard-sounding word to some, we use it to emphasize the importance of listening to God in the group.

When we describe each group as unique, we are hitting a key point. It is very important to recognize the uniqueness and to listen to the group. When we don't do this, problems will occur.

3

And Many Adopted Cousins

What's different about an intergenerational small group? The answer for us goes back about five years. That was when we started such a group in our church. We wanted our children to experience, as we were experiencing, the open, and supportive life-style of small groups. We needed an "extended" family. We wanted our children to experience love and affirmation and support from other adults. We wanted for them, and for us, the reality of open, straight communication with persons of all ages.

The group lasted a year. Then we joined a group made up of several families, from three different churches, and with ages ranging from five years to the fifties. We have a preschooler, elementary age, teens, singles, and couples in this family. We meet once a week, varying the time. We vary the agenda with a wide variety of activities. Some are serious, some are pure play. We try to keep a good blend in order to experience all of family life. Sometimes we do a Bible study, using role-playing to get ourselves into the story. Often our activities lead naturally into deep worship experiences.

No Different

We are no different from other adults, nor are our children really different from other children. People

Of prime importance is the fact that, in an intergenerational group, we are doing things *with* our children rather than *for* them.

everywhere can experience what our group has. It isn't difficult, and the results can be fun and result in growth. There are, however, some differences between intergenerational groups and other kinds of small groups. We suspect that a bit of knowledge about these differences will be helpful to you.

Of prime importance is the fact that in an intergenerational group, we are experiencing it *with* our children rather than *for* them. The kids are full participants in the group. They are important as persons. Their ideas and suggestions are as valid and needed as those of the adults. It's so easy to try to "lay something on" the kids, to talk down to them so they will understand. Children read emotions far more accurately than most adults. They know when someone is talking down to them, and they don't like it anymore than an adult likes it. What a child has to say is important, whether it is a suggestion, an idea, or a need. In talking with the younger children, it's important to get on their eye level. When talking with them, we spend a lot of time on the floor. Little things make a big difference in the quality of communication.

As equal partners in the group, the children often volunteer to lead a particular activity. We need to give them the freedom to try it their own way. We haven't had any real failures of leadership. The children bring a freshness, and a trust when leading, that adults need to rediscover.

In the group process, we do need to be aware of children's limitations. We can give them more responsibility than they are capable of handling. That will cause problems, and we need to be sensitive to the danger. At the same time, we want them to make choices and to be responsible for their choices. We want to expect of each person in the group, child and adult, all that their individual potential and personality can offer.

The Scriptures describe the family of Christ as having different parts. All of the parts are essential to the health of the body. Children are some of the parts, and their full participation is necessary for the family health. People of all ages tend to live up to the expectations of others, so why not expect good things? Children and adults will respond to positive expectations with positive actions.

Flexibility

When children are involved in a small group, flexible programming is essential. Kids can handle much "deeper" talking than we give them credit for. Sometimes we do need to be careful in our choice of words, but kids can grasp some very significant concepts. Age is a factor, obviously, but don't sell them short. Like most adults, children also need some fun time. An adult can go longer on discussions than a child, but a blend of activities is important. Deep sharing and understanding can come from playing together as often as it can from talking together.

We have found that a worship time is a strategic part of each get-together. Some of our most creative and meaningful worship times have come as a part of a fun-and-games outing. Worship does not have to be a quiet, somber time. It may be, but it may also be a celebrative, joyful, loud time. We can celebrate the good news with laughter, shouting, and running, as well as with prayer and meditation. However it develops, we have chosen to include a "centering-in-with-God" time in each of our group meetings. It may be only five minutes, or we may devote the entire meeting to worship. No, it's not always easy. But we believe it is important, and it can be done. And it's important enough to make the effort.

Handling Interruptions

If you have worked with children, or have your own, you know that there will be interruptions. The same is true in a group. If you have a low tolerance for interruptions, try another kind of group.

There are some pluses to this side of an intergenerational group. For example, spontaneity comes with interruptions. That is a creative way of saying that we are never sure what is coming next from the younger ones. Some-times it's irrelevant, but sometimes we get a new perspective on things through the eyes of a child. Be open to it. Another learning value comes from how interruptions are handled. A quick "no" or "stop that" is a put-down, a discount of the child as a person. But by expecting and asking the children to be responsible for their own needs and wants, we can help them learn how to ask in straight language. They interrupt because they want or need something. If a child can learn to say "I need" or "I want" instead of the more common ways of being disruptive, he has learned a valuable lesson in interpersonal relations.

Well, it sounds great in theory, but what do you do with a noisy four-year-old who doesn't know what being responsible means? For one thing, love him. Also, try to have some toys or games they can go play with when they get bored with the group activity. We have found that the younger children will move in and out of the group as their attention span varies. That's OK. Let them wander in and out. Most important, listen to them and respond to their personhood.

Older Children and Youth

For the older children and youth, the problem of interruptions can be handled a bit differently. We ask **31** ours to make a choice to participate or not participate when we are involved in a sharing activity. We ask them to be responsible for making the choice. We try to let them know that we want and need their participation, but that we can also understand if they prefer to do something else while we are talking. If they choose not to participate for that sharing time, they agree not to interrupt those who are involved. Again, this encourages them to become responsible for their behavior and also honors their right to make decisions. Adults take note—this applies to us, too. It takes a liberal amount of common sense and sensitivity to the child, but it pays off in kids that are aware. To say it another way, let's learn to accept what a child has to offer in the way the child can offer it. How often adults miss the gift of a child because it wasn't offered in the form or words that adults expected. One significant way to love another person is to accept gifts as given within their limitations. That's true of all ages. In the intergenerational group, learn to expect the unexpected, and beautiful things will happen.

When starting an intergenerational group, you need to talk about how to handle behavior problems in the group. For example, my child may be doing something that I do not notice. Another adult in the group may be bothered by it. How will the group handle this? Our way has been to give each adult both the permission and the responsibility to correct a child in the group when needed. We try to do it caringly, stating that "I am getting angry because the noise is preventing me from hearing what is going on. I need for you to sit down." By taking responsibility for our own feelings and needs, both adults and children learn how to communicate more accurately. This is an area that will need *clear* understanding in your group. A lot of very strong emotions are involved in how our children are corrected, so be sure to get this clarified in the beginning.

On the positive side of the group parenting question, it is great at times to have other adults take over our parenting role for a few minutes. A special example of this happened one weekend at the beach. When you mix a curious four-year-old with the waves, undertow, jellyfish, and other pleasant beach attractions, you have a ready-made disaster waiting to happen. Constant watching by mom or dad (or both) is a must. Unless you really get your kicks from being a lifeguard, the constant alertness can get old. It's nice to have one of the other adults in the group offer to watch while you go for a walk or swim. For us, that turned a nerve-racking day into a real fun time. It also gave our child some special time with another adult who cares and loves her.

Evaluate Periodically

Normally, when we train group leaders, we suggest they stop after a year together and evaluate where they want to go next. They may want to continue for another year. After two years together, we suggest they stop. We feel the family group is an exception to this. The group should periodically evaluate where it's going, but it can go on longer if it wants. Families don't cease after a couple of years, so neither should the intergenerational group. Also, as the children grow and mature, the group changes. We are not suggesting that a group go on forever. When it loses its meaning and importance to the members, stop! Keep asking yourselves and the group what's happening. And be honest about it.

A word about group size. We suggest small groups limit their size to twelve members. For the intergenerational group, we have found that eighteen can be handled, if several are children. We will say more about that later.

By now you may be wondering if you really want to try this kind of group. Fear not—read on. True, the intergenerational group does require some different approaches and skills. But they aren't that different. Common sense, sensitivity, and loving concern will go a long way toward ensuring an exciting, growing group or family.

4

We're Always Growing

Life is a never-ending growth process. As we grow our needs develop and change. Knowing the variety and changing of needs is an important part of understanding what happens in an intergenerational group. Volumes have been written on the developmental process, so we will hit only the main points.

The variety of needs adds greatly to the excitement and growth potential in an intergenerational group. It doesn't happen the same way in an adult-only group.

The Infant

Let's start with the infant. Needs at this age are simple and easy to understand. Warmth, love, and nourishment—that's it. Obviously, a baby cannot "participate" in the group activities in the ways we usually think of. They can contribute, though. A baby brings to a group the gift of new life. Physical and emotional growth are rapid in these early months, and the group can actually see a life growing. And babies are a lot of fun. They do interrupt. Their needs are immediate and must be met *now*. At times scheduling group meetings may need to be adjusted for the baby. Group support of the baby's parents can be important during this phase. Raising babies isn't easy!

As the infant reaches the crawling and exploring phase, around six months to one year, the group's tolerance for interruption will be tested. Expect it, and try to have some interesting things for the "explorer" to do. The group is still giving more than it's receiving from the youngster, but a one-year-old is certainly cute. This is the stage in which some basic programming (TA term) starts. This early programming can be very difficult to change later, and the group can provide some valuable positive input. For example, if the child learns that adults and other children are warm and friendly and loving, future relationships will be easier and more healthy.

As the child moves into the toddler phase, he begins to give the group a model of trusting curiosity. The "little professor" reads the feeling thermometer of the group and responds. He also begins to reach out to adults other than mom and dad, and to respond with love and warmth. Keep the toys handy and the breakables out of the way. Expect the interruptions to continue.

Through these early years up to age three, there will be times when the group needs baby to be elsewhere. That's what baby-sitters are for. Don't feel that the group has to receive baby's gifts at every meeting. One big word of caution. The teenagers in the group are part of the group. Don't expect free baby-sitting. That's not fair to them, and the group will miss their participation. We're not saying teens or other adults should not help with the playing and rocking—if they choose to. Just be aware there will be times when toddlers should be left at home with a sitter.

The Preschooler

From age three to five, the child rapidly becomes a social being, relating to others better and being able to
 receive more. Though they may not grasp concepts, they

will pick up and respond to expressed feelings. For example, when our Mende was just three, we were leading a family retreat for our church. Because of our leadership role, we were not sure whether to take her. We chose to take her, though the wisdom of that was questioned when her daddy was interrupted in midprayer by an insistent, "Daddy, I gotta go now!" What else can one say except, "Thank you, Lord, for children's freedom to state their needs—Amen!"?

During this retreat, we grouped natural families into clusters to form extended families. We did some sharing and getting acquainted. During a free time, Mende fell and skinned her knee. She was hurting and frightened and looked for one of us. Not finding us, she saw the other daddy from our group and ran to him for comfort. For us that was a solid affirmation of the process. Even though Mende didn't understand what we had been sharing in the group, she had experienced the feelings of closeness that had developed. She knew that other daddy was someone special who cared.

The preschooler will wander in and out of the group. Just expect it and have a room or a corner where he can go to play when he tires of the group activity. Give preschoolers the freedom to be who they are. When they do choose to participate in a group discussion, you may be in for a surprise. At four or five, they begin to grasp concepts of things like death, convenanting, choosing.

Early School Years

As a child moves into the grade school years, changes significant to the group begin to develop. This is the phase in which a child wants to join groups and identify with groups. They become legalistic with a strong sense of right and wrong. By age seven, they begin to express **37** their values and can participate in values clarification exercises. They want to compare the life-style of their own natural family against other families. Hero worship starts during these years. They are able to participate in group discussions, and they often bring unexpected insights of great value to the group. They can begin to accept limited leadership and planning responsibilities. They can both give and receive affirmation. They can make choices on their role in the group. The group in turn will meet many of the needs of their age, providing the care and support relationships.

Early Adolescence

Next comes early adolescence, roughly the years from age eleven to fourteen or fifteen. This age child begins to look for alternative models from mom and dad. Other adults in the family group are prime candidates. The early teenager tends to have a low self-esteem, to look for ways to feel good about himself. Affirmation from the group is very important. This age often has difficulty verbalizing ideas, and a great amount of patience and understanding may be needed in relating to them. Nonverbal exercises are helpful in guiding the child through this difficulty. If you have tried to buy clothes for this age, you know it is a period of rapid physical growth. You will also see a growing awareness of sexuality. The early teen may need an adult other than mom or dad to talk to. The group can be particularly helpful in giving the teenager the permission to make choices, state needs, and be responsible for who they are. This is a trying age both for the child experiencing it and the adults around him. The child usually has trouble relating to adults. The group can help the child grow through these times. We have been especially pleased to see our own thirteen-year-old able to relate openly and warmly with adults, both in and outside of the group. Because adults in the group have listened, supported, and affirmed him, he has the self-confidence to reach out and share with others. The early teen can give more to the group, accepting his part of responsibility for the group.

High School Years

Now let's talk about teenagers in the high school years. This age gets a lot of bad press around the country, sometimes even in the church. They don't deserve 99 percent of it. Contrary to popular opinion, teens are people, too. For the family group, expect some rebellion. The teen is becoming an adult, and is trying to become an individual apart from his natural family. Teenagers need to try new ideas by thinking for themselves. Yet while they are rebelling and moving away from mom and dad's control, they still want and need the security of a family structure. The family group can provide this alternative structure. This need may bring a teen into the group without his natural parents. Allow the teen to ask the tough questions and give him an honest answer. They can smell a phony in a second. Listen carefully and don't be shocked if a teen questions the reality of God. If, as Catherine Marshall says in one of her books, "God has no grandchildren," this questioning is important to the teenager. Out of it they will find their own personal faith. Give them plenty of tender, loving care, but also give them space to be.

Young Adulthood

Adulthood arrives at last, age eighteen—twenty-five. These are the years of moving out of the childhood home, becoming independent and legally free to do as one chooses with one's life. It can be a lonely time for the person away from home for the first time. The supportive relationships in a family group help ease the lonely feeling. The intergenerational group also provides a chance for young adults to relate to younger children in a close way before having to face the task of parenting.

Though not as universal as it once was, somewhere in the mid-twenties, marriage comes along. Beyond that comes parenting. Mixed in all of this is the work of merging life scripts with the spouse and with society. Eagerness and enthusiasm for life are characteristic of this phase. Sharing the growing and exploring with a family group can add much to both the young couple and the group. For the young parents, group support can be especially strategic, providing a time of relationships in an otherwise tied-down phase.

Single parents will find a family group helpful in several ways. The single parent will usually be a mother with children. The adult men in the group can provide a male model for the children. For the mother filling her dual role of mother, father, and wage earner, the emotional support of a group is needed. In a similar way, the single father with children will find a group helpful.

Median Adults

As adults, single or married, move through the twenty-five to fifty years, they will recycle through some of the earlier phases. Regaining the freedom to play, reprogramming old tapes that are no longer valid, learning to share with others—these are needs that will affect the group.

Older Adults

Beyond age fifty, the person reaches some new phases of life. For the couple with children, these are the years when the children leave or have already left the home base. This can be a severe period of adjustment. There are also the years in which the working person accepts realistically the limits of his career. The experience of the years brings maturity that can be a big plus to the family group. Looking forward to the retirement years enters the picture. Accepting the realities of life and relationships may be easy, or it may be traumatic.

For the children in the group, contact with aging may be available nowhere else. We are a youth-oriented culture, and our children may not have a chance to be with people beyond the fifties in their neighborhood or church. Grandparents often live too far away for frequent visits. The process of aging is a natural, healthy part of life, and we should want our children to experience others in this process. We have found this in the intergenerational group.

Bringing Church Members Together

In a couple of churches we have worked with, the intergenerational group has offered a new way to bring church members together. These are churches with a large number of members over the age of fifty. Both are large, old churches located in downtown areas of the city. Their younger members, families with young children, have been leaving for the suburbs. They are using intergenerational groups as one way to reverse this trend. We believe this can offer many churches a new option in strengthening their congregational life.

In some ways each age and stage is unique, yet all are **41** common in one need. We all need much tender, loving care. We need to be affirmed for who we are. We need for others to listen and hear what we say. We need to love and be loved. We need to be needed. We need to share our lives, our dreams, and our fears with others we trust. We need to accept others as they are, accepting their gifts in the ways they are able to give them.

From birth to death we grow. That's good news!

5

Take Me to Your Leader

The style of a group leader goes a long way in enabling or disabling group process. By saying that, we are disagreeing with those experts who claim that anyone can lead a group. Perhaps anyone can, but some do it far better than others. Our experience proves there is no such thing as a leaderless group. Lest you get ahead of us, the one exception will be a group in which most or all members are experienced in group process. In most situations, however, a group needs a leader. In fact, if the group does not name a leader, someone in the group will emerge in that role. It may never be officially acknowledged by the group, but it will happen. Think back about groups you have been in, and you will see what we mean.

Leadership Styles

Let's talk about leadership styles and what we see as important. In a small group (including the intergenerational group) the leader is first a participant. He or she leads by doing, by modeling. He is neither a facilitator nor an observer. If the leader communicates an attitude of "This is a great activity—*you* do it, and *I'll* watch," the group is handicapped. When you are sharing a special part of yourself, do you want an uninvolved observer in the group? Of course not. We each want to know we can **43** trust the others in the group to hear us with genuine concern and involvement.

The leader sets the tone by his level of openness and sincerity. By sharing at the level with which he is comfortable, he invites others to do the same. This establishes a feeling of trust as the group grows together. To expect others to share more than you are willing will guarantee problems and limit progress. We will go one step further. A group will go no farther or faster than its leader is willing to risk himself. Sounds heavy, but it's true.

Any volunteers to lead a group? Having emphasized strongly the importance of the leader, we also want to say that it is not as awesome as it sounds. The main thing a group leader needs to do is to be sensitive to each person in the group and to be aware of where he himself is. Most of us, perhaps even all, have a deep inner need to share with others what we are thinking and feeling. Group leaders are people with the same needs as anyone else. Be yourself.

44   **Effective leaders let others see and hear their inner feelings.**

Just as the group will go no farther than the leader is willing to go, it will also go no farther than group members as a whole are willing. If you try to lead a group into a subject it is not willing to deal with, the group will not respond. We saw a good example of this recently. The group leader wanted to move into a sharing of feelings about death. This group, which had been very open and talkative, suddenly grew quiet. No amount of coaxing or personal modeling by the leader could get them going. It was either too painful or too scary to deal with, and that group just would not talk about it. As a group leader, you will know when this happens. You can feel it! Don't force it. Be flexible and change your agenda.

As a group leader, you are not responsible for the group's progress. The group is responsible for its growth. As a participant, you share in that responsibility, but it is not totally yours. It is usually helpful to get this clearly understood. It is easy to assume that kind of responsibility, and it is a heavy load if you do. In fact, it is an impossible load. You cannot do it, so don't try to be a hero. If a group is not willing to take responsibility for its growth, then maybe you need to ask yourself if you want to be a part of it, let alone lead it.

Let Things Happen

So much for the negatives. By being a participant yourself, an enabler, you can let things happen. Most of the really beautiful happenings we have experienced in groups were not planned. They spontaneously grew out of some activity with a purpose completely different from what actually happened. Lyman Coleman calls these "serendipities," chance, happy happenings. It's like watching popcorn pop. You know something is about to happen, but you don't know which kernel (or person) will be the one. You cannot make it happen. You can let it happen. You can be part of it. You can be yourself.

By far the most effective leaders we have seen were the ones who were willing to let others hear and see their inner feelings. Some call this leading from weakness rather than strength. We prefer to call it leading from reality, from personhood. Yes, it is weakness because we all have weaknesses. It means being vulnerable. That is not easy because sometimes vulnerable people get hurt. They also experience being accepted for who and what they really are. That experience is what Christ promises us. And it is worth the risk.

Leadership Tasks

A group leader does have some specific tasks or roles to fulfill. One of these is to ensure that everyone's rights are protected and honored. Every person in a group, regardless of age, has a right to share or not to share—to "pass." That person may feel a strong pressure to share, especially if everyone else has. But it is OK to pass. The group leader needs to ensure that everyone knows this and honors this.

Many of us get uncomfortable quickly when silence drags on. As group leaders, we need to learn to be comfortable with silence. Make yourself a mental sign that reads "QUIET—GOD AT WORK." In these moments of silence, redemption may be happening. Avoid jumping in too soon to break the silence. On the other hand, do step in and restart things if the silence becomes awkward. Trust your own feelings to tell you when that happens. Our own inner feelings can tell us a lot if we will listen to them.

46

The Need to Confront

Because we have all learned so many games to use in hiding our true feelings, a leader may need to confront an individual at times. This must be done gently and with loads of love. A good way is to ask the person, "What do you need from me (or the group)?" To confront someone does not mean to pry. Remember, everyone has a right to pass. By confronting, we ask another person to be accountable for his needs and behavior. We ourselves may need to express the anger or hurt we are feeling because of another's words or actions. Do it by saying "I am feeling anger because . . . ," rather than "You make me so mad!" Yes, that's playing with semantics, but it is also a lot more. It's acknowledging that we are responsible for our feelings. By his own model, the group leader can enable others to confront openly and honestly.

Confidentiality

For any group to grow in trust, confidentiality is a must. Everyone must understand that what is said in the group remains in the group, unless specific permission to share with others is given. Adults often forget the significance of this with children and discount their need for it. Repeating what a child has shared in trust and confidence will destroy the trust level and seriously damage the relationship. The same is true with adults. As a leader, make sure you emphasize this point. We know of a couple of instances in which a parent shared some feelings and concerns about his children (this was in an adult group), only to have another group member repeat it to the child. It wrecked the parent-child relationship for several months. When others share their inner feelings with us, they give us a priceless gift of themselves, and we must respect and **47** protect that gift. Treat each such gift with tender love and care, for the other person is trusting you to do so.

Finally, the leader needs to make sure the housekeeping details get taken care of—things like time, date, and place for the next meeting. Make sure the group is aware of special days like birthdays. Call the group to a periodic evaluation of its purpose and future. There will be other details that need attention. We are not suggesting that the leader must personally do all of these, but rather to make sure someone is doing them.

Above all else, remember to be part of the group rather than above it. No two groups are the same, and they will each respond differently and uniquely to each situation. Only when you are part of the group can you be aware of these responses. So, experience it fully, just as you hope the others will. Trust the Holy Spirit to guide the group. He will!

6
Group Life

The most frequent question we are asked about intergenerational groups is how to get one started and how to keep it going. What kinds of things do you do? While we can and will share our experience with you, the main thing you need to do is let your imagination loose. Everyone of us has a built-in creativity given by God. It enables us to know our needs and find ways of meeting them. Daydream, let your ideas spring out. Don't be afraid to try something in getting a group started.

Get Started

To get started, talk with your own spouse and children and decide what you want and need. Then try to think of others you know who may have similar needs. Work with a total group size of not more than eighteen. Try as much as you can to include at least three generations—children, adults in the twenty-five to fifty age range, and adults over fifty. Ask some single adults to come. Singles are very much a part of God's family, yet too often we exclude them, or they exclude themselves when we use the word family.

One of the really special things about forming a family group is the choosing. This is not an excluding type of choice, but rather a positive exercise of our freedom of **49** choice. We get to choose the aunts and uncles, cousins, etc., for the family.

One word of caution is appropriate. For some reason, church people get nervous when a new group forms in their midst and they aren't asked to be in it. To avoid that, put an announcement in your Sunday bulletin or weekly newsletter. Invite any who wish to participate to call you. Not only do you keep everyone aware of what you are doing; you may also get some totally unexpected interest. If you wind up with too many people for one group, form two, or three.

Even with the official invitations in the bulletin or newsletter, you still need to call people personally. There's just no substitute for the personal touch. If you get a balanced group from the invitation, great. If not, get on the telephone.

One of our tendencies when trying to start a group, for whatever purpose, is to call these individuals or families who are already involved in church life. That is a good way to miss some strong possibilities. Our churches are full of spiritually and relationally hungry people who simply don't know how to get involved. Either that or they are afraid. So take a chance and call some of those people who aren't very involved. See what happens. Your pastor may have some suggestions. Oh yes, be sure to let him know what you are doing. You are not asking for permission— but you are keeping him informed.

OK, now you have some names to contact. You have scheduled a time and place. What do you say when they answer the phone? First, tell them what you want to do and why. Ask them to come to one meeting and try an experiment with you. The best way to explain this kind of process is to personally experience it.

Bruce Larson tells a story in the June 1973 issue of *Faith* *at Work* magazine that illustrates this. It's about a turtle named Charlie. One day while driving to work, Bruce found Charlie crossing the highway. He picked Charlie up and took him to the office for the day. Well, Charlie enjoyed quite a day in that cool, air-conditioned office, sampling tidbits from everyone's lunches, and listening to soft music. That evening, Bruce took Charlie back to the highway and sent him on his way. Imagine the difficulty Charlie had trying to explain to his turtle friends where he had been all day. We humans are like that—it is hard to understand something we have not experienced.

In your first contact, you just want to get people to try an experiment with you. If you get a few "no" responses, try some more. You don't have to limit it to your own church, either. Try neighbors, friends, other churches.

There are a couple of other good ways you may want to use in starting the group. One way is to ask one other

To sum it up in three words, if everyone in the group can *pray*, *play*, and *participate* together, the group will become a real family.

family or individual to join you. Then the two of you choose a third and ask him to join. Then the three of you choose, and so on until you have a full group. A second way is to introduce a large number of folks to intergenerational methods at an evening celebration at the church. This makes a super program for a family night supper. We have used several of the designs from this book for these evenings. At the end of the evening you can invite those who are interested in a continuing family group to meet with you.

Any of these will work well, so look at your situation and pick the one that is best suited for your needs and go with it.

Let's talk about the first group meeting. You want this to be a good experience for everyone, so we suggest some light, history giving exercises. Use one given in this book or a similar one. Lyman Coleman suggests a lot of these in his books. You may want to try one of them.

Fast-paced, Please!

For that first meeting keep it light and fun and fast moving. Oh yes, if you or someone in the group plays a piano or guitar and can lead singing, that's a great way to start the meeting. Singing helps to set aside the inner agenda everyone comes with and gets everyone to a common place. Keep your meeting length to an hour and a half, or less. And remember what we said earlier about having a play place the younger children can go to if they get bored and need a change.

To close the meeting, ask how many would like to continue meeting regularly as a family. Then set the time and place for the next meeting and stop for the evening. Juice and goodies (cake, cookies, etc.) at this point will go a long way in helping the children and some adults decide it is worth doing.

Now you are on your way. For the first few meetings, six or eight, continue the history giving. Include a picnic or an afternoon at the lake or beach. By the fifth or sixth meeting, you may want to try an affirmation exercise. These are powerful trust building times for a group. To hear yourself and your children affirming and being affirmed by others is a great feeling. Parents see their children as extensions of themselves, and being affirmed by children is special.

After six or eight meetings, we suggest that the group devote one full session (two if necessary) to talking about where you want to go next as a group. You may want to write a specific covenant for the group, stating the guidelines by which the group will function. We strongly urge you to have a written covenant.

To use our own group as an example, we have a written covenant. At the end of every 3 months we have a planning meeting. We all bring our personal calendars with us. We spend a block of time brainstorming to develop a list of possible activities for the coming quarter.

Brainstorming

The brainstorming is an important time, worth a few specific suggestions. Brainstorming means to think of ideas and state them, regardless of how impossible or impractical they may sound. One idea may not be possible, but it may trigger an idea in another person. This kind of sharing of ideas very often produces some beautifully creative suggestions. A key point to remember in brainstorming is that *all* ideas are valid. Write them on a piece of newsprint so everyone can see them. If one of the children suggests a ski trip to Alaska, write it down. It is very easy and very damaging to discount a child's ideas in this exercise. Obviously, some ideas are not practical, but review that after the brainstorming, not during it. For more information on this technique, we suggest the book, *Values Clarification*, by Simon, Howe, and Kirschenbaum.

After developing the list of possible activities, we go through the list and select those the group wants to do. Next we select dates and times for each one. We also individually volunteer to either host or lead one of the activities so that each planned event has a designated leader or leaders. The leader is responsible for making whatever arrangements are needed. He or she also makes sure a worship time is planned.

In planning activities, we find it is easy to schedule an entire quarter of "doing" things. This can be a mistake. When we are busy doing things, often we are not able to really sit and talk to each other. So, we include at least a couple of "sit and be" times in our schedule. These are times in which we plan no activity and just talk and share with each other. These have been some of our most significant and growing times as a group. Be sure to include some in your group.

In addition to leaders for each event, we also have two leaders (we call them priors) for the quarter. The priors coordinate any schedule changes during the quarter, ensure that birthdays or other special days are celebrated, and provide overall leadership for the group. The children take their turns at this as well as the adults. We do avoid having two children priors in a quarter. We don't want to give the children more responsibility than they can handle.

Recommitment

 When all of this planning is completed and everyone

has agreed, we have a time of recommitment. Each person in turn states his choice or decision to commit himself to the group for that quarter. This may sound very formal and legalistic, yet we have found it to be both important and deeply meaningful. We do not take each other for granted, and the rededication is our way of verbalizing this to each other.

During this committing time, we can also make any special requests or commitments to the group. For example, faced with a job change, one member may request special support and prayers during the transition. We are a family, and we do call on each other for support and help.

As a group we struggled through the first few quarterly planning sessions. It is not easy to coordinate eighteen different sets of needs and schedules into one common plan agreeable to all. But it has been worth it. Through these meetings, we have experienced conflict, and we are learning how to handle it more creatively.

We feel that this method of planning and committing to each other has been a key part of our group experience. It does take effort, and it requires a strong commitment to each other and to the process.

In the quarterly contracting sessions (we call them contracting rather than covenanting) we often discover unexpected learning opportunities. One in particular happened recently. All of our decisions are made by consensus. We define that to mean that all group members must agree before we will go ahead. On one activity we had a seventeen for, one against, vote. The one was Tim, who is eleven. As we talked further, Tim became aware both of his individual power and also his responsibility to the group. He shared with the group his awareness of this. Through his awareness and his freedom to talk about it, we all became more aware of our own power and responsibility to each other.

A word about frequency of meetings may be helpful. We meet once each week, and we urge you to. If that is not possible, then meet at least every other week. To spread the time between meetings beyond two weeks simply will not work. To grow as a family, the group needs frequent times together, just as any small group does.

We have looked at getting the group started and talked about the importance of a specific covenant. What can you do to keep a group healthy and going strong?

Christ-centered

To begin, we are a Christ-centered group. We have already talked about including some kind of worship in each meeting. Worship and prayer can be in many forms, some quite different from the commonly understood meanings of these words.

In whatever form, be sure to include worship and prayer in your group. Build around it. Let the Holy Spirit lead. Listen.

Work and Play

Both for the adults and the children in the group, keep a balance of work and play. We all need some of both. Our American culture and religious work-ethic have somehow convinced many of us that play is not necessary, a waste of time. We wind up being very serious all the time.

If there really is a little child within each of us, as suggested by TA, that child needs its share of our time. Jesus himself talked about coming as a child to him. We believe he meant that we need to regain the simple faith and trust of a child. We have discovered that playing together in the group brings us closer together. It also builds the trust level, and our faith and trust in each other open the door to deeper faith and trust in God. When we play together we relax emotionally. We share our fun side with each other and with God. We celebrate the fun and beauty of God's creation.

Look at God's world through the eyes and wonder of a child. It is fascinating. Instead of seeing just another bird, you will see the color, pattern, and beauty of a cardinal or a robin. When was the last time you really looked at a cardinal? Look at the flowers, trees, sky, and animals. Some are really funny. God must have a great sense of humor to have created some of the weird creatures we see. Yet each is vital to life. Give yourself the freedom to laugh, roll in the grass with the kids, let a child *take you* for a walk. Play leapfrog if that sounds like fun, and laugh with God.

As you laugh, you may also begin to cry. The release of long controlled emotions can be both frightening and healing. Another thought from Lyman Coleman—have you ever noticed how thin the dividing line is between hilarity and healing? From the very serious to the beautifully ridiculous is but a laugh or two. We believe Jesus laughed often. To be full of joy and at peace with who one is cannot help but give rise to genuine laughter and celebration. It's exciting and it's healing.

A balanced amount of work, or serious, time is equally essential. One of the surprising and exciting discoveries of our family group experience is the depth at which young children can share and participate. The key to unlocking their participation has been assuring them of their worth and equal partnership in the group process. Once they know we really do want to hear their ideas and feelings, and that the adults will not discount them, children are eager to share. They have a much greater capacity to understand and comprehend than most adults can acknowledge. This is particularly true when dealing with something at a feeling level. Children may not always grasp the intellectual concept, but they rarely miss the feelings that are communicated. We have observed that anytime our group is dealing with feelings, the children stay with us. They only get bored when we get into intellectual discussions.

Group Intimacy

We would like to say a word about intimacy in a group. Our American society has convinced us that physical touch is not OK, especially between men. As a group grows closer, wanting to hug each other will naturally occur. Do it! In almost all of the healings recorded in the Scriptures, we find that Jesus touched someone as part of the healing. Holding hands or a warm hug in a group is both significant and important. It is tremendously healing in relationships.

We are also finding that intimacy develops in different ways in a group. Sharing deep fears and feelings with another is an intimate sharing. So also is two adults delightfully laughing and enjoying the funny animals and creatures in the nocturnal animal building at the zoo. When two adults care enough and trust enough to share their little child feeling, there is intimacy. For some of us, we need to consciously choose to allow others to get close to us. A lifetime of "be strong" and "big boys don't cry" injunctions has isolated us from each other and from ourselves. Choose to let others be near you, and let yourself be close to others. It is a great way to grow as a human being.

Accountable to One Another

58   Accountability and responsibility are also important

words in group process. In a family group, we are accountable to each other and to God. We need to make those important choices that keep God at the center, that enable us to gently confront when necessary, and to forgive. True forgiveness is so important. Forgiveness from another person is vital to healing and building quality relationships. We are going to hurt each other at times. It is unavoidable in close relationships. We have a responsibility to work through these hurts and to forgive both ourselves and each other. In a group, we need to be willing to feed back to each other what we are hearing and feeling. We have Jesus' life as a model to follow. He confronted others, at times gently, at times not so gentle, but always with love and a willingness to forgive. This is yet another area of learning that children give us. Children's feelings are close to the surface, easily hurt. But given a genuine "I'm sorry—will you forgive me?", a child quickly forgives and forgets. Isn't that what Jesus tried to tell us? God forgives quickly, and he doesn't keep score on us. In the story of the prodigal son, the father forgave. If that same son had repeated his act of going away, would the father again forgive? Unless we have really missed the point of the story, the father would forgive seventy times seven times.

Learning to accept forgiveness is the tough part. Children do it quickly, adults are not so able. A story illustrates this point. A man in his prayer to God said, "God, do you remember that sin I talked to you about yesterday; the one I asked your forgiveness for?" God answered, "No." God does not keep score. When he forgives, he forgets it. Children can help show us adults the reality of that in a group.

Sensitivity

Keeping a group strong and healthy requires sensitivity

to both self and the other group members. As the group relationship becomes more important to you, it becomes more difficult to say "My needs are not being met." Yet that's exactly what we must do to keep the group strong. If we control the negative feelings, we will also control the positive feelings, and the family loses some.

To sum it all into three words, if everyone in the group cay pray, play, and participate together, the group will become a real family. The results will be fun and will result in support and growth for all.

7

From the Mouths of Babes

For us, this is the most exciting chapter to write. We want to share with you some of the insights that have come from the children in the group. Some are funny, some are profound. All are precious.

Young children bring a fresh sense of wonder to a group. Their simple trust and faith in life are contagious. They bring to a group gifts which adults have lost. By being free to play, they give us permission to play again. A moment of play is as necessary to our emotional health as vitamins are to physical well-being. A child's enthusiasm is contagious—it rubs off. Their way of sharing deep truths, of "telling it like it is," reminds us of Jesus' words: "Whoever does not receive the Kingdom of God like a child will never enter it" (Luke 18:17, TEV). Those words hold deep meaning for us.

What Happens

So much of the faith of adults today gets all wrapped up in intellectualism. When we talk about the Bible and its meaning, big words are called into action. Adults seem to need to impress each other. All too often we get so busy with our words that we forget to listen to each other. We forget that Jesus lived simply. He spoke in parables that the uneducated fishermen and farmers could easily un- **61** derstand. He spoke in language even a child could understand. Something interesting happens when children are part of a group. Adults simplify their language so the children can understand. And all of a sudden the adults begin to understand each other, perhaps for the first time.

Children also have a way of asking the innocent, penetrating questions that adults are either afraid to ask or have forgotten how to ask. A child can ask a question in a manner that demands a straight, honest answer. He wants the answer simple and to the point. Kids can sense a phony answer in an instant.

A Sense of Wonder

Young children inject a special sense of wonder into the group. On one of our group outings (which we called "Sister Sylvia's Sensuous Saturday") we spent an evening exploring the fountains, stores, and underground tunnels

 Little children can also teach us what trust really means.

of downtown Houston. Mende, age four at the time, helped all of us discover the beauty of a tiny flower in a sidewalk crack. She was fascinated by such common things as grates and manhole covers. Through her we all rediscovered the beauty of design and function in these otherwise unnoticed bits of God's world.

On that same outing, as we were walking through the underground tunnels, someone said, "Wouldn't it be fun to play leapfrog in here?" Before we knew what had happened, the kids started it, and the rest soon joined in. Away we all went, much to the amusement and puzzlement of others walking by.

Little children can also teach us what trust really means. One evening, George (one of the adults) took Mende by her hands and twirled her around and around in the air. As she soared through the air, she laughed, opened her eyes, and completely relaxed. Because she trusted George so totally she was free to experience a new sensation of motion and feeling. From that we all realized that a freedom from fear, which includes a deep trust, is necessary for us to experience soaring with God and with each other.

A child's ability and freedom to fantasize, to imagine, often give him an intuition and perceptiveness that is profound. Matt, our ten-year-old, described one of the adults in the group in a way that was full of insight and deeply moving. His explanation was that she was like a salmon, fighting upstream against the flow of life, searching for her destiny and meaning. Mike, at age thirteen, described another adult as a dolphin—beautiful and intelligent, so much so that he didn't always understand what she was saying, even though he knew it was important. Again, it was an accurate insight.

Children can also confront others more openly and directly than adults seem to be able to. One evening Mike was leading a group discussion, but all of the adults were engaged in one-on-one, talking and paying no attention to him. He finally shouted to get everyone's attention, and then said, "I am angry! If I were an adult, you would be listening. I feel discounted and hurt, and I'm mad!" We all learned an important lesson that night about respecting each other, regardless of age.

We have discovered that our children are able to handle topics for which we thought they were too young. On a family retreat a year ago we were doing a group exercise, using drawings which we made that dealt with life and death. Death is a tough topic for adults to handle. Yet Mende was able to join in the discussion and contribute in a way that none of us expected. Another "serendipity" happened that evening. Barbara, who was leading that part of the discussion, sensed in Mende's words an unnatural fear or guilt. Later, she took Mende for a walk and the two of them talked about death. Mende was feeling some painful guilt over the death of a pet guinea pig several weeks earlier. Because of Barbara's sensitivity and willingness to accept Mende as a person, our daughter was able to deal with death in a healthy way. How much better to do that at age four than at age thirty-four.

Matt came up with a fascinating observation of our group during a weekend retreat. We had asked everyone to draw a picture that said something about where we each were with the group. He drew a maze of freeways. In explaining it, he said we were all going places so fast we were like cars on a freeway. Because we were going so fast we weren't seeing each other. We could not even see the exits where we could get off. At that point in our group life we were all growing rapidly and were very busy going to seminars, leading retreats, working, etc. Matt helped us see that we all needed to slow down a bit and be with each **64** other more fully.

We often get into the Bible through relational Bible study and role playing passages of Scripture. Here again, we have received a gift from the children. In the role playing, adults are very reluctant to play the part of Jesus. Even though he promises to live within us through his Spirit, we are not comfortable assuming his role. Children are free to do it. They will volunteer to be Jesus quickly and eagerly. They bring a freshness and vitality to the role that must surely make him happy. One example occurred at a church celebration in which we were involved. In one learning center we were role playing Jesus' first meeting with Zacchaeus. A tall daddy was playing the part of Zacchaeus and was standing in a chair (trees aren't easy to find inside a church). Along came the four-year-old son of our pastor. Jay was playing Jesus. He stopped and looked up in the "tree" and said, "Hey Zacchaeus, what'cha doin up in that tree?" The daddy answered according to the Scripture. Jay replied, "Well come on down. I'm hungry so let's go eat at your house." He paused, and then added, "You do have peanut butter and jelly, don't you?" Jesus may or may not like peanut butter, but he does meet people with that kind of openness, acceptance, and simple faith.

Children love to try something new. On our trip to Astroworld the children were first in line for the Texas cyclone, a huge roller coaster that is scary to look at, let alone climb into. Their excitement and expectancy rubs off. Up and down and around—just like life. Can we approach the ups and downs of life with that kind of excitement and eagerness? And then get off at the end saying, "That was fun; let's do it again." We surely hope so. Besides, as Mende said, "Sometimes it's fun to be a little scared."

As we have written this book, we have continually asked our boys Mike and Matt to read it and give us their **65** input. They have done so with eagerness and have been a great help. Many ideas and methods throughout what we are saying have come from the boys. We feel this really affirms our belief that children can be in a group, participate fully, and contribute to its growth and success in ways that adults cannot.

We are grateful and thankful for all the children and what they have given us in this process.

8

Loving Someone Means Having to Say Good-bye

Contrary to popular belief, loving someone really does mean having to say good-bye. Groups do not go on forever, and the way endings are handled is important.

We became very aware of this after one of our family group meetings. We had been to a pizza place for supper together. Some of the group had to leave early, and our time together ended vaguely as people left. It just faded away. Our boys were quiet on the way home. When we asked if there was a problem, Matt replied, "I missed saying good-bye." Both boys expressed a sense of something incomplete about the meeting.

Endings are often painful. Yet we need to deal with them. There is a sadness in parting, even if you are going to see each other again next week. We have found it important to have a defined stopping time, and to give everyone a chance to say good-bye to each other. That closure is needed. To deny that is to deny a part of life itself. By including this in our group life, we can help both children and adults learn to accept and deal honestly with parting.

This becomes especially significant when someone leaves the group. This will cause painful feelings, sadness, and a sense of loss. When this happens give yourself permission to feel and experience the grief. Plan an evening of celebration and parting before the person(s) **67** leaves. Celebrate the good times you have had together, remembering the fun and special moments. Then say good-bye. Tears communicate love as well as grief, so they can be shared also.

As in any family, serious illness or death within the family group will be tough. Yet the opportunity for sharing and growth is great in these crises. To be able to say to someone in grief, "I care" is a deeply meaningful and supportive expression of love. We know of a group in the Covenant Church in Redwood City, California, in which a mother died. The group was able to grieve with and support the family in the loss. Experiencing the grief process together was not easy, but the family and the group were able to come through it healthy and strong.

When a group begins to lose its reason for existing, and groups do, the ending can be a long, drawn out failure or a specific, clear ending. If your group reaches this point, don't let it fizzle out or fade away. Plan a special time to

By saying good-bye, we can help both children and adults learn to accept and deal honestly with parting.

celebrate what the group has meant to each other, and let that signify the death of the group. There is nothing more smelly than a walking corpse. Have the funeral and bury it! Do it in a specific, clearly understood celebration. And then go on to life's next experience. In this sense, a family group is more like a group than a family. At the same time, however, the relationships from the group do not end. They continue, just as our natural family relationships do when we leave home for college or marriage or whatever. Celebrate and rejoice in these relationships. Treasure them. And be open to meeting new people, new places and new experiences. Only when we say good-bye to the old can we truly be open to the new.

9

Covenants

Covenants are not a new idea in the Christian world. God made convenants with Abraham early in Genesis. He made one with Noah. In the life and resurrection of Jesus, we have the New Covenant. So, it is a concept as old as man's relationship with God. Through his Spirit, Jesus is a part of the family group covenant. We hope you will establish a specific covenant for your group. We feel it is important enough to include a chapter on the how and why of covenants.

Why a Covenant?

Why have a written covenant? People come to a group, any group, with all kinds of needs and expectations. They are often unaware of some of these. The process of preparing a covenant does two things. It enables a person to think through his needs and expectations and thereby clarify them. (You can't write them down if you don't know what they are.) By discussing these with others in the group, you are also communicating to them (and them to you) what your expectations are. If we know what your needs are, we are better able to meet them. This will also go a long way in preventing future misunderstandings. The group may decide that it cannot meet certain needs or expectations. It is a lot better to know that at the beginning than to painfully discover it after six months of struggle.

If everyone, children and adults, knows their own needs and expectations and can clearly state them, expect no problems. However, in this real world we live in, you will not find many of any age who can do that. We do not always know what our needs are. Often, a vague, uneasiness about something is a symptom of an unmet need, but we are not really sure what it is. To compound all of this, our needs change as we grow. This suggests that the first covenant your group writes may need changing. If so, do it. Covenants are to enable, not disable.

Why write it down? We often hear people object to the written covenant as being too rigid and legalistic. That will happen only if you allow it. Writing it helps clarify the covenant and also provides a good reference when the group needs it. It provides structure for the

Put some genuine thought and time into the covenant your group uses.

present as well as a known point from which changes can be made later. Make sure everyone in the group has a copy.

In writing your covenant, keep it simple. It is not a legal document nor should it be a monument to someone's mastery of big words. The children need to understand it as well as the adults.

Covenants can talk primarily about housekeeping details or they can talk about commitments to each other, or both. Examples of each type follow. We have also included an exercise we used to help a group develop a covenant. Another description of how to write a covenant can be found in the October 1975 issue of *Faith at Work* magazine. Look on pages 19 and 20.

The covenant is important and helpful. Put some genuine thought and time into the one your group uses. Give yourselves the flexibility to change it when needed.

SAMPLE COVENANT

1. We will meet weekly. The family is important to me. I will give it high priority and try to come to each meeting. I will notify the hosts if not coming.

2. We will renew our contract quarterly.

3. Consensus

Decisions must be made by consensus (unanimous). In order to facilitate this process, no major decision can be made unless every member of the group is present. Otherwise, it is the responsibility of the priors to see that each absent member is informed of the question at hand and has an opportunity to voice his or her opinion by the next meeting.

4. Priors

Two members of the group who volunteer to be responsible for the planning of the group's schedule for one quarter. Other responsibilities include keeping a record of decisions made by the group and notifying absent members of impending decisions.

5. Convenors

Each meeting will have a person labeled the convenor who will be responsible for acting as a clearinghouse of information about that particular meeting, such as time, place, what to bring, etc. The convenor is also responsible for acknowledging in some way the birthday of any member whose special day falls within the preceding week. Birthdays are times of special celebration. It is also the responsibility of the convenor to decide in what manner we will worship during the meeting.

6. Leaders

The leader has the responsibility for the main content of the meeting. He may or may not be the convenor for that meeting. Leadership will rotate among the group.

7. Children

Some part of each meeting will be set aside for special emphasis of being together as a *family* and having fun together as a whole group. We will make a special attempt to involve the children in the activity and plan for their interest level. If the children wish to play elsewhere, they may do so. However, if they participate in the group activity, we will expect them to fully participate.

8. Grown-up Share Time

We also recognize that the grown-ups sometimes need to share things with each other that may not be appropriate to share with the children. Therefore, the adults feel comfortable in claiming a certain amount of time to themselves when the children are asked to entertain themselves elsewhere and not interrupt. We will try to set the time period so that children will be clear about how long they will be expected not to interrupt. This time limit will be flexible to the needs of the individuals in the family. We will therefore feel comfortable in requesting a longer period of time if the circumstances of the moment require it.

9. Size of the Family

Since this is an attempt to be a family to each other, we feel a need to set a definite limit on the size of the group. We have decided that _____ is the maximum number a family can have and still be able to develop and maintain some intimacy within the group. Therefore, membership in the family is now closed. At the start of any given quarter it may open again, but only if some members decide not to renew their contracts for that quarter.

10. Visitors

As in any family, we will occasionally want to bring friends or house guests to a family gathering. Some gatherings will lend themselves to the incorporation of guests more readily than others. That decision is up to the persons involved. However, it is the responsibility of the family members involved to inform their guests that the group is no longer open to the incorporation of new members. If someone is interested in the extended family concept, we will be happy to encourage them and assist them in starting their own extended family.

EIGHT PRINCIPLES OF COVENANT GROUPS

(The following principles are not legalisms. They are simply principles and guidelines that represent where some of the people at National Presbyterian Church in Washington, D. C. are. They were drawn up by senior pastor Louis Evans, Jr., and are printed with permission.)

Covenant Groups are an expression of our life in Christ, and cannot reach their potential unless he is an active member of the group. Our life and strength flow from Him; therefore we can take joy in His presence and express what He is accomplishing in our group as a member of it. His Word is our guide to all of life and therefore it should be used as the group feels the need. It is out of His Word that we identify the following covenant dynamics:

1. The covenant of Affirmation (unconditional love, agape love).

"There is nothing you have done, or will do that will make me stop loving you. I may not agree with your actions, but I will love you as a person and do all I can to hold you up in God's affirming love."

2. The covenant of Availability.

"Anything I have—time, energy, insight, possessions— are at your disposal if you need them. I give these to you in a priority of covenant over non-covenant demands. As part of this availability I pledge regularity of time, whether in prayer, or in an agreed upon meeting time."

3. The covenant of Prayer.

"I covenant to pray for you in some regular fashion, believing that our caring Father wishes His children to pray for one another and ask Him for the blessings they need."

4. The covenant of Openness.

"I promise to strive to become a more open person, disclosing my feelings, my struggles, my joys and my hurts to you as well as I am able. The degree to which I do so implies that I cannot make it without you, that I trust you with my needs and that I need you. This is to affirm your worth to me as a person. In other words, I need you!"

5. The covenant of Sensitivity.

"Even as I desire to be known and understood by you, I covenant to be sensitive to you and to your needs to the best of my ability. I will try to 'hear you, see you and feel where you are,' to draw you out of the pit of discouragement or withdrawal."

6. The covenant of Honesty.

"I will try to 'mirror back' to you what I am hearing you say and feel. If this means risking pain for either of us, I will trust our relationship enough to take that risk, realizing it is in 'speaking the truth in love, that we grow up in every way into Christ who is the Head.' I will try to express this honesty, to 'meter it,' according to what I perceive the circumstances to be."

7. The covenant of Confidentiality.

"I will promise to keep whatever is shared within the confines of the group, in order to provide the 'permissive atmosphere' necessary for openness."

8. The covenant of Accountability.

"I consider that the gifts God has given me for the common good should be liberated for your benefit. If I should discover areas of my life that are under bondage, 'hung up,' or truncated by my own misdoings or by the scars inflicted by others, I will seek Christ's liberating power through His Holy Spirit and through my covenant partners so that I might give to you more of myself. I am accountable to you to 'become' what God has designed me to be in His loving creation."

COVENANTING

Objective

The objective of this design is to introduce covenanting to a group. Most group members, especially first timers, have not been exposed to this part of the group process and are often uncomfortable with it. This design provides an easy and fun way to get into the process.

Materials Needed

Newsprint and a magic marker.

Time

About one hour.

Instructions

Divide the group into subgroups of four to six. Then:

1. Remember back to your childhood years (which can include up through high school if you need to). Who was the most significant "best friend" you had in those years? The children in the group can answer also. Share with the group who that person was and the kinds of things you did together.

2. Describe as best you can remember them the qualities that drew you to that person. Another way of asking this is, "What did you particularly like about that person?"

3. What are the qualities in you that drew your friend to you? In general, what do you like about the way you relate to others?

4. Along with the things you do well, you have certain needs and wants. State three needs which you want this group to meet. What do you want the group to be and do? When working with children in the group, we want to encourage them to honestly state their needs and wants. You may hear some statements like: "It's hard for me to sit still for long periods." "When you adults get into long discussions, it gets boring." "We want the adults to play with us kids some." "I want the group to be more spontaneous." These are normal, natural statements for a child, and we want to both encourage them and give them the permission to share their real feelings.

5. Bring the subgroups back into one group. Ask each person to quickly share what his or her three needs are. Write these on the newsprint. Then, as a group, look at the list of needs and wants. Discuss for clarification if needed. Consolidate the needs as appropriate, and then negotiate an agreement on a group covenant.

The covenant should be periodically reviewed to be sure everyone is still satisfied with it. This can be done quarterly, semiannually, or once a year.

10

Now That You're All Together

We are often asked, "What kinds of things do you do in your family group?" Looking back over two years of meetings, we are amazed at the variety. Where did all those neat ideas come from? In almost every case, the idea grew out of some particular interest, hobby, skill, or knowledge of someone in the group. We talked earlier about the 'brainstorming' process we use. That environment brought out some innovative and new ideas, and from them came the activities and events we have done as a group. We want to share some of these with you, but first let us talk about what makes a good meeting design.

Just Visit

For every group meeting, allow some time at the start for people to visit with each other. It has been a week since the last time you were all together, and you need to check in with each other, find out what has happened in the past week. People do this naturally, so expect it and allow time for it. You may want to do some type of "ice breaker" game. In whatever form, this getting started helps each person set aside whatever agenda they came with. That's important. The planned activity for the meeting will go a lot better if everyone is fully participating. So take some time at the beginning to come together, set aside prior concerns and worries, and be fully with each other. After two years, our group needs this as much as ever.

Each meeting should have a stated program or activity scheduled. Ideas for these will come from the brainstorming session. Sometimes the program may be simply to be together with no agenda. That's fine as long as everyone knows it ahead of time and comes expecting it.

An Activity

The planned activity should be something everyone can participate in. If it is an "adults only" kind of thing, the children will feel left out and will be disruptive. So don't schedule something that excludes the children unless they specifically agree to it. In two years with our family group, we have done that only once. The older children agreed to it and were given the option of participating. They chose not to. During the planning of events, if someone is really uncomfortable and does not want to be part of a particular event, find something else.

A big item in planning any kind of family activity is the family budget. So it is with a family group. Be sensitive to each other's financial limitations and avoid putting undue strain on group members' pocketbooks.

Each group meeting should have a designated leader. Someone needs to be in charge to make sure planning and arrangements are taken care of. Rotate this task among all the group members.

On Time

Maintain a group discipline of starting and stopping on time. If some of the group have to drive farther than the 79 others, an occasional late arrival is likely. The visiting time at the beginning of the meeting provides some cushion for this. If you know you are going to be late, let the leader know. If you know you will have to miss a meeting, let the leader know, also.

We have some "bread breaking" together at most meetings. It may be a full meal or it may only be snacks or refreshments. The importance of this is easy to forget, yet it is a significant part of family life. Families eat together. We also find many references in the Scripture about people eating together. Many of the stories of Jesus being with people are around a meal. We believe that is significant, and we urge you to include it in your planning.

Finally, and most important, include some time in every meeting for worship, for checking in with God. It can be brief, it can be unconventional. But be sure to plan it into every meeting.

  Worship can take many forms, as in this *agape* feast.

Two other suggestions may be helpful to you. In your planning, a time limit of an hour for discussion is about as long as you will want to go. Even if you are on an all-day or weekend retreat, limit the discussion time to an hour. Both children and adults get restless at that point. You may want to schedule several one-hour discussions over a weekend. That's fine, if you space them with fun time in between. Also, an individual group member may come to a meeting with a need that is more important than the planned activity. Have the flexibility to set the agenda aside to meet that need. That is what families are for, to support and help each other in times of need.

Group activities fall into several types according to the purpose or objective of the activity. Early in a group's life, you will want to focus more on group building, history giving, and getting to know each other. Later, after you have been meeting for several weeks, you can add more variety to the menu. In your planning, try to keep a balance of activities, including some from each type. The types of activities we use are:

1) *Group Building/Maintenance*

These are activities that get the group to first and second base. History giving and trust building are the main objectives. These are two of the three most important types of activities a group does. (The other is worship.) Getting to know each other is essential. In a family group, both children and adults are growing and changing, so you need to continually get reacquainted. For group building, go more with "where I've been" questions. In doing these history giving exercises, have the adults answer from their childhood, and have the children answer from the present. This does two things. First, it frees the children from having to answer the same way their parents do. Second, it provides the children with a different view of their parents. Parents were once kids, but our children rarely see this part of us.

One of the get-acquainted questions we often use is to describe your favorite hiding place when you were a child. Our children still get a real kick out of hearing their mother talk about hiding in the dirty clothes hamper. You may also get some unexpected answers, like the twelve-year-old in one of our groups who said, "If I tell you where my favorite place is, then it won't be my secret place any more!" She didn't tell us, either. And that was OK.

For group maintenance, go to the "where I am" and "where I want to go." Ask questions like "What is the most significant or exciting thing that has happened in your life this week?"

There are many ways to build a group and maintain one. We have tried many including:

* Any of the history giving/getting acquainted exercises suggested by Lyman Coleman will work well. Use his ideas as a starting place to think of your own design. Try it and see what happens.

* Slides/Home Movies—Spending an evening sharing family slides, pictures, and home movies introduces the family group to our larger natural families (parents, brothers and sisters, cousins, etc.) You may also want to include any slides or movies you have taken of family group events.

* Affirmation Exercises—These will do wonders for a group. Use both self-affirmation and affirmation of each other. One way is to ask each person to tell the group what he likes about himself for one minute. Then, have the group respond for one minute with things they like about that person, a strength bombardment. Ask the person being affirmed not to talk—just listen. What a great feeling this can give you. Other exercises from Serendip-ity are the animal, color, or gift giving affirmations.

* Gift Exchange at Christmas—Plan a special evening together to celebrate Christmas. Draw names for the gift exchange. Limit the cost per gift if you need to. Some may want to hand make their gifts. These moments of sharing become very special memories. You can also make it an educational evening by talking about Christmas customs of other lands or of each natural family. When you exchange the gifts, have one person start by presenting his gift. Let the receiver open it and show it to the group. Then he presents his gift, and so on around the group. It takes longer one-by-one, but it gives each member the group's full attention in turn.

* New Year's Eve (or anytime) Slumber Party—Have everyone bring sleeping bags and all sleep in the living room or den. It is great fun and provides an extended period of time for getting acquainted. With everyone pitching in to help with dinner and breakfast, it is just like a family reunion.

* Weekend Retreats—We will cover these in detail later. They provide lots of time away from life's usual interruptions where a group can really focus on each other.

* I Remember When—Good for special times like family group anniversaries. Spend some time recalling memories of the group's together time over the last year.

* Sit and Be—This is an evening with no planned agenda other than being together. Take some time to visit with each other, or play, or whatever your need is.

* Sing-a-long—An evening sharing favorite songs brings the group together. Ask each person to explain why they like the song they picked.

* Any Holiday Party—Valentine, Halloween, and July 4 are all good times for a party together. Build it around the theme of the holiday. Include some discussion about how the holiday fits with Christianity. Valentine is a

sharing of love. Halloween came originally from a church holiday. July 4 is a celebration of freedom. In the group, explore what the customs mean.

* Church Calendar—The church year is full of special days which we are often not familiar with. Build an evening of sharing around the theme of each one.

* Family Birthdays—These are special days for each group member. Schedule several times through the year to celebrate birth dates. At the meeting day nearest a person's birthday, have everyone sign a birthday affirmation card. On it, say in writing "I like you because. . . ." Bake a cake, celebrate with each other.

* Fruit Picking—If orchards are near you, check with the owners to see if they will let you pick some fruit. That can lead into a neat worship experience built around the Scripture passages on harvesting. Any activity in which the group works together helps to build a group.

* Preparing a Meal Together—Whether on a picnic or in someone's home, this offers growth from working together.

* Working Together—Helping someone move or paint their home are work projects that can be lots of fun and at the same time build a family. There are many possibilities with this basic idea. Working together and meeting each other's needs are important ways to develop close relationships.

2) *Worship*

Though we are repeating, this is important, important enough to include it in your planning. Do it in whatever form meets your group's needs, but do it. Make God part of the group. Build around his presence.

Within your group are lots of new and interesting ideas on worship. You will find new questions and new ways of looking at things that can open worship experiences for you. Do not get locked into roles or definitions or ways of doing things. Be flexible and expect the unexpected. Spontaneous worship experiences can happen when least expected. For example, while we were flying kites one afternoon, we were talking about the wind lifting the kites up. Someone noted how it was like lifting each other up. From there we moved into a really special sharing of faith. If you trust each other, and if you are truly open to question and share your hopes, dreams, hurts, and questions—worship comes naturally and often.

Worship comes in many forms. Here are some we have used.

* Role Playing—Role playing a Bible passage can be an exciting worship experience. It offers a way to express feelings in which all ages can participate. Role playing is one of the most creative group activities. By combining the techniques of relational Bible study and role play, we can really step into the Bible and claim its message for ourselves. It can also be fun. One great example came when Matt transformed the feeding of the 5,000 into an evangelistic crusade in the Astrodome. Fish and chips became the available food. Irreverent? Not really. He simply put the story from the Bible into a familiar setting, and in so doing gained a new understanding of the miracle of Jesus. Better to be slightly irreverent at times than to be completely irrelevant.

* Relational Bible Study—This method is great for personally getting into the Scripture and finding a message for each person, a personal message.

* Walk in the Woods—This can be worship, by being aware of God's creation and its complex and fragile beauty. Compare that to the beauty in each group member.

* Parts of a Worship Service—Subdivide the group and have each subgroup examine part of a worship service (call to worship, music, message, Scripture reading, etc.). Plan and have a service with each subgroup leading their

part.

* Singing—Sharing religious music is always good. Look at both contemporary and traditional music. Compare the words and melody. Using rhythm instruments, you can involve everyone in both playing and singing.

* Easter Sunrise—Plan a special sunrise time together to celebrate this event. Have breakfast together afterward.

* Bible Meal—Plan a meal together using foods from the Bible, (figs, dates, nuts, etc.—sit on the floor).

* Foot Washing—Jesus gave us this model of serving each other. For a group, it is a powerful and beautiful experience. Combined with a meal and love feast, it offers a unique way to experience one of the Bible's most significant passages.

* Love Feast—Throughout the Bible are examples of fellowship at mealtime. Using a loaf of bread to symbolize the shared love within the group, celebrate the unity with each other and with Christ.

* Explore Contemporary Writers—A good way to gain some new perspectives on Scriptures is to review contemporary writings. *The Narnia Tales* of C. S. Lewis; *Way of the Wolf* by Martin Bell; Wes Seeliger's *One Inch From the Fence* and *Western Theology, Cottonpatch Theology* by Clarence Jernigan; *The Parables of Peanuts* by Robert Scott—all are ones we have used. Do not forget secular childhood books, many of which have a message for all ages. Examples are *The Velveteen Rabbit, Whobodies, George and Martha,* and *The Little Prince.*

* Nonverbal—Pantomime and similar nonverbal methods often introduce a new look at Scripture or song. Acting out a passage of Scripture without any words is both challenging and interesting. This is yet another activity in which children, with their freedom and lack of self-consciousness, can enable adults to participate more

fully.

These are some ideas on how to design an entire meeting for worship. We also want to include some brief worship in every meeting. How do you have a worship time in the midst of thousands of people at a large amusement park? With a little ingenuity, you can find ways. At the amusement park, as an example, you can sit down together at a picnic table or any convenient place and reflect on the importance of play in our lives. How would Jesus react to a modern amusement park? Or, you can talk about the contrast of reality versus illusions. Talk about the feelings of fear caused by a roller coaster ride, and how such feelings are handled.

One of our fun times is to eat at ethnic restaurants. We have tried Chinese, Greek, Mexican, German, and local Texan restaurants. Take a few minutes during the meal to talk about the people and country represented by the restaurant. Remember that all people are God's children, and be thankful for that.

A trip to the beach offers all kinds of possibilities. The perpetual waves, the sea from which God created the first life on our planet, the variety of sea life—all can lead into a sharing and worship time. Or you can build sand castles, noting how the waves sweep them away. Jesus talked about building on sand and on solid rock. Where are the sandy areas of your faith, and where are you on a firmer foundation?

We have taken trips with our family. One was an all day ride on a passenger train. You can tie that to the many biblical stories of families traveling. Note the differences in traveling between then and now. We have also taken a pilot boat trip on the Houston ship channel. Here the group talked about our need for a pilot for life, for a navigator for our lives. Jesus can be that navigator.

If your group is at a zoo, take a few minutes to talk about

the variety of life forms. Looking at some animals, like an elephant or giraffe, we become more aware of God's sense of humor in his creatures. Creation, the story of Noah, and animals in the Bible are all ways to get into worship.

One of our more unusual outings was a visit to a large, old cemetery. As we walked among the headstones, we met many of Houston's early citizens. It offered a chance to be in the presence of death in a comfortable way. A mother mockingbird teaching her youngster how to fly told us that life goes on. We talked about Jesus and his friend Lazarus, about death and resurrection.

Worship can take many forms. From simply enjoying the beauty of the world to a deep sharing through prayer, God has given us many ways to be in relationship with him. All of these are worship if we will be aware of what is happening. We are not suggesting these as replacements for formal worship in a church, but rather an expansion of worship into all of life. No matter where we are or what we are doing, the opportunity for worship is always present. Look around you, experience the moment, and celebrate it with the group and with God.

3) *Going and Doing and Celebrating*

Every family we know likes to take trips and go places—to the beach, on a picnic—things like that. Family group outings are lots of fun. Sharing the excitement and discovery of doing and seeing new things adds to the fun. These activities are so popular, you may find your group wanting to do them all the time, particularly in the summer months. Be aware of this tendency. Don't overdo it to the point you spend all your time going and doing and forget to be.

The variety of things to do and places to go is limitless. Your only concerns are time and money. Planning is the key to having a successful outing, so be sure to involve the entire group as much as possible in the planning.

Here are some of the outings we have taken over the past couple of years.

* Art Show—Galleries and sidewalk art shows are popular in the Houston/Galveston area, so we have had several opportunities to visit the world of art.

* Tour of Rice University Campus—The architecture of the buildings on campus tells a fascinating history of the university. One of our group is a Rice alumnus, and George guided us on this one. After the tour, we visited the chapel for our worship time.

* Ethnic Restaurant—Can be both educational and lots of fun. In larger cities, you will find plenty.

* Breakfast in the Park—A variation of the familiar picnic. Plan an early morning breakfast in a park or anywhere else you might go for a picnic. Follow it with some games involving the entire group.

* Boat Tour—Most seaports have sightseeing tours by boat. Some of these are free. Check around your area to see what is available.

* County Fairs—Every community has one sometime during the year.

* Renaissance Fair—These are becoming more popular around the country. They offer a look into medieval history that can be quite entertaining and educational.

* Octoberfest or Fiesta—In areas of the country with strong ethnic backgrounds, you will often find annual festivals celebrating customs from the "old country." In Texas, both the German and Mexican influence is celebrated. Check around your area.

* Hiking—Most state and national parks have nature trails for the public to use. This form of outdoor exercise and fellowship is great for group building.

* Sailing, Boating, Canoeing—If any of your group has the equipment, these activities are lots of fun. Try combining it with a picnic or backyard barbecue or shrimp

boil.

* Bicycling—Good exercise, good fellowship.

* Ice-skating—Here's a good one, regardless of where you live. Rinks are becoming available even in Southern and Western areas. Hilarity follows quickly after you step on the ice for the first time. If ice rinks are not available, try roller-skating.

* Zoo—Every child we have ever met loves the zoo. When adults can allow their inner child to be free, the zoo becomes an enchanting place in which you travel across our entire world.

* Candlelight Tour—In Houston, a small park in the downtown area holds homes and shops from the city's early years. The homes are opened for tours during the Christmas season, and are decorated and lighted authentically for the period. Traditional Christmas foods are prepared over open fires and are available for sampling. For our group, the trip downtown helped to bring Christmas '76 alive.

* Train Ride—If you are lucky, you may be near a tourist railroad using steam locomotives. Whether modern or old, a train ride is still a special treat for all.

* Crabbing, Fishing—If you live near the sea, crabbing may be of interest to you. A string, hunk of old meat, and a net are all you need. And crab is a delicious meal.

* Symphony, Museum, Planetarium, Observatory—Any of these places provide opportunities for group activities which you can use.

* Miniature Golf—Pure play.

* Theater—Houston is fortunate to have a large outdoor theater used for musicals, drama and concerts in the summer months. And it's free. See what's available near you.

* Amusement Parks—More and more are being built

 around the country. If there's one near you, take it in as a family.

* Beach—A trip to the beach or lake is always fun. It can be anywhere from a half day to an entire weekend. Most state and national parks have camping areas if that's your thing.

* Fruit Picking—Be sure you have permission before doing it.

We could go on and on. But we would rather you use these suggestions to get your thinking going and see what you can come up with. There is so much to see of our country, of God's natural world, that you won't lack for opportunities.

You do not have to go somewhere to play. Play can be planned for a living room or backyard. A family softball game can go on a vacant lot. Kite flying requires only some open space and a little wind. Frisbees are great backyard toys. You can also go back to your childhood, remembering games you played as a child. Lead the family in playing them again—Kick the Can, Hide and Seek, Mother— May I. Yes, adults can still do these things. And when you do them all together, adults and children alike reach a common level of being. That's important for both children and adults. Sure, you may feel a bit silly at first. So what. Be with the children on their level, and you may find a special part of yourself that you haven't been in touch with for many years.

4) *Creating*

We have found that every person has an inner creativity that wants to be expressed. One of the great joys of a family group is calling forth these creative gifts and celebrating them together. Children are real enablers of this process with their freedom to try new things. A fascinating dynamic occurs when children and adults create together. We first saw it verbalized in a book by Jack and Sherry Rodgers called *The Family Together*. Have you **91** ever noticed when adults are asked to draw a picture for a history giving exercise we quickly say things like, "I'm not a very good artist," or "I can't draw very well." We unconsciously start competing with each other. Introduce a child into the group, and the competition stops. What adult will try to compete with a child? With the competition gone, the adults are free to try new things, often with surprising and delightful results.

Creating can sometimes get a bit messy, so be sure your host for these activities feels OK about messes. Some don't, and we need to honor that. This is also an activity in which group members can share their creative gifts with each other. You will find artists, singers, musicians, outdoor and camping enthusiasts, super cooks—you name it—in a group of fifteen to twenty people. Asking someone to share their skill with the group strongly affirms them. On the other hand, a shy person may be reluctant to try a new skill or share one that is not perfected yet. A caring and supportive group can encourage and give permission to be less than perfect. You may also find your own hidden talents emerging and developing. That's just plain fun!

Some of our group creations have included:

* Painting T-Shirts—Using acrylic paints and fabric markers, we created our own personalized T-Shirts. The results were definitely original art.

* Poetry Writing, Reading—Several in our group shared poetry they had written. Others read poems or writings they found especially meaningful.

* Paint a Fence—Tom and Marsha have a large board fence around their backyard. At their suggestion, we spent an afternoon creating a pictorial graffito on their fence. Even the grass got painted.

* Face, Body Painting—At one of our Halloween parties and again at our Mardi Gras celebration, we painted each other's faces in lieu of masks. Much fun. Be sure to

use a water base tempera paint that will easily wash off. The world may not be quite ready for permanently painted faces. On our beach retreat with everyone in swim suits, we tried body painting. Have you ever had a daisy painted on your left knee?

* Talent Sharing Night—Devote one evening to a family talent show. We enjoyed everything from a record pantomime to a very first guitar solo. Can you think of a better place to show off your new talents (or even some old ones) than with your family? Especially talented families may need two or three nights to work everyone in.

* Play—Last year during the Christmas season the group went to the outdoor theater on an afternoon when nothing was scheduled. We created a Christmas play spontaneously. We unexpectedly drew a spontaneous audience, and everyone loved it!

* Banner or Quilt—One of our most successful group projects was our family quilt. Everyone created it, and it is on the front cover of the book. If you don't want to try something that elaborate, make a family banner.

* Family Album—Creating a family photo album is a great way to keep a pictorial history of your life as a group.

* Family Movie—If you really want to try a large project, make a family movie. Many people today have movie cameras that are easy to use. You don't need sound, though you can have it if you wish. Some of the group can be cameramen, some script writers, editors, even a director. Plan to do it over several months. We have been working on ours for a year now and we still aren't ready for the local theater.

* Family Scroll—Take a large roll of heavy shelf paper. At each meeting, whoever wants to can write a few words on it, or draw a picture. Looking back over a year's worth of graffiti gives an interesting group history.

* Family Collage—Here is another group creation

that's fun and helps build the group. Each individual finds words and pictures that express what the group means to him. These are all glued together to form a collage. Matted and framed, it becomes a very interesting piece of family art.

* Folk Dance—You can spend an evening folk dancing. If someone has a friend who can show you dances from other countries, invite them. One of your group may be able to do this.

5) *Expanding Our Awareness*

These are the activities that get a group to third base and on to home plate. Life is full of experiences that we either are not aware of or that we take for granted. Looking as a group at some of these can open new understandings and insights of both the world we live in and the potential God created within each of us. Looking at our emotional reactions to situations helps us understand our feelings. We all have needs, and by becoming aware of them, we can find acceptable and healthy ways of getting them met.

Our American culture has many phrases that can lock us into roles. We have all heard of "women's intuition." Most children have a keen intuition. Why can't men have it? Men can. How about "big boys don't cry," or "men aren't afraid." In reality, big boys do hurt, and sometimes need to cry. And men can be very afraid. Have you heard many Christians voice doubts in their faith? Not many, because doubts aren't permitted. Yet we all have doubts at times. We all have questions. Through group activities, we can ask questions or voice doubts and fears. We believe that's important. Some ways we have used are:

* Tree Climbing—With a trained and qualified resource person leading, we used rope ladders and lines between trees to climb and move about. Safety harnesses were used to ensure no one could fall. Even knowing that,

it is a strange feeling to walk across a rope between trees depending on the others to support and guide you. A similar experience can be gained in rock climbing or rapelling. After it is over, talk about the feelings you have experienced. CAUTION: Please *don't* try these activities without an experienced and qualified leader. We do not want anyone to get hurt. Properly supervised they can be exciting adventures. If you do not want to try this, go for a roller coaster or ferris wheel ride.

* Sister Sylvia's Sensuous Saturday—Sylvia planned this one—hence the name. We spent an evening exploring the underground tunnels of Houston. It's explained in detail in another chapter.

* Massage—A good back rub can do wonders for one's morale. Some of the basic massage techniques are simple and easy to learn. They help us get in touch with our physical responses to tension and fatigue. Helping another to relax is a way of caring, and expressing that care in a demonstrable way. It is a strong nurturing kind of activity.

* Mardi Gras—By having our own family Mardi Gras celebration, we were able to explore a part of church history and tradition. We talked about the meaning of Ash Wednesday and all of the events which are part of the Lent season. This party is also playing and celebrating.

* Field Day—An afternoon of athletic games helped our group gain an awareness of the priceless gift God has given us in our bodies. Strength, speed, agility—we each have these in varying degrees. Friendly play and teamwork bring the group closer together, too.

* Halloween Party—This one was neat fun. We all dressed up in costumes, created after we got there. We also had a "haunted room." Getting in touch with childhood fantasies and fears was great fun. We even turned out all the lights except one candle and told ghost stories. **95**

* Affirm America—This was a short time together at the end of a July 4th spent sailing and playing together. The purpose was to do an affirmation exercise for America.

* Simulation Games—There are lots of these games available in group dynamic books. Some can be used very effectively in family groups to help us understand both ourselves and the ways we relate with others. The real learning value from these is in the debriefing after it's over. Be sure to allow plenty of time to talk about the experience.

* Nonverbal—These help us use senses and communication skills other than voice. We also become more aware of and sensitive to body language and how others respond to it.

* Relational Bible Study—There are three excellent resources for this type of activity. One is a book by Dr. Karl Olsson called *Find Yourself in the Bible*. Lyman Coleman uses lots of relational Bible study in his Serendipity books. Wally Howard, editor of *Faith at Work* magazine, frequently includes Bible study suggestions in the magazine. The beauty of this approach to Bible study is that the questions deal with how you personally respond to a passage. You don't get all wrapped up in theological doctrines or stands. This works great with adults and children. We highly recommend it.

We have given you lots of ideas from which you can develop a program for an evening. You might like to see how we have actually developed some, so we are including a few. These will focus on one thought or theme. They can be used in a group, in a Sunday School class, or as an introduction to intergenerational groups in a training situation. They take from an hour to an hour and a half to complete. They can also be used as the nucleus for a larger celebration, or several could be combined into a series.

Childhood Night

This design was written by the children in our family group; Mike and Matt Henry, and Tim and Judy Lawson (with a bit of coaching from the sidelines). It combines history giving, nostalgia, and play into a fun and enjoyable evening. The children led the events, giving the instructions and calling time as needed.

Objective

The objectives of this design are to enable the group members to get to know each other and to learn to play together; for the adults to get in touch with the natural child in each of us; to give the children an opportunity to lead the group for an evening.

Materials Needed

Balloons, soap bubbles, jacks, similar toys and games, paper, and pencils for each person. Also, each person is asked to bring a baby picture of themselves to the meeting, not letting anyone else see it. Each person is asked to bring their favorite childhood toy, if they still have it. They can describe it if they no longer have it.

Time

About two hours.

Instructions

1. As each person arrives, they are given balloons, soap bubbles, or jacks, depending on which they want to play with. (A large patio or backyard is very desirable for this part of the evening.)

2. When everyone has arrived, start playing some childhood games in the backyard. Drop the handkerchief and Mother-May-I are a couple of suggestions. Have the children select the games before the meeting.

A variation of this approach would be to let each person pick a favorite game and lead the group in it. For the adults, remembering childhood games can really be fun. **97**

They can briefly tell the group why it was their favorite and then show everyone how to play it. The children would use current games for this, or perhaps ones they played when they were younger. As we talked about this in our group, we rediscovered the special joy and magic of playing kick-the-can at dusk on a warm, summer evening, hoping mother won't call us in for bedtime. The children enjoyed these as much as the adults and were surprised to learn that some games have been around for a long time. The children also gain self-confidence by teaching the adults how to play some of the games.

3. The next activity is "guess who this baby is." The baby pictures, which everyone brought with them, are placed around the house (kitchen, family room, living room). Each one is numbered. To add interest to the game, some pictures can be placed in hard-to-spot places so that you have to look for them (a sort of hide-and-seek). Ask each person to make a column of numbers on a sheet of paper, from one to nineteen (or however many you have in your group). Then everyone looks at the pictures and guesses the identity of that person, recording the name beside the number on the list. When everyone is finished, see how well each did. In our group we thought we really knew each other and were surprised at how many misses we each made. The scores were low, but the hilarity level was way up.

4. Next ask everyone to share their favorite toy. It was surprising in our group how many still had those old toys. Each person can in turn explain why this toy was or is special. It was really neat when Mende discovered the fifty-year-old celluloid doll, and Frances discovered a new doll that can eat, sleep, cry, walk, and even mess in its pants (all of the things we have finally gotten Mende beyond). As we relived childhood memories, and the children shared new feelings, our commonality and

closeness grew.

5. To close the evening, talk a few minutes about the Scripture passage in Matthew 18:3. Discuss what it means to "come as a little child." Talk about the differences between childlikeness and childishness.

6. After sharing, have each person create their own special sundae and enjoy refreshments together.

Note: This design was particularly significant for us in the way it affirmed the children. It also enabled all of us to get in touch with our own inner child. Our first steps as a group in this relearning were both hilarious and healing.

The Truth Shall Make You Free

The design on p. 100 is based on the Johari Window and the Scripture passage "Know the truth, and the truth shall make you free" (John 8:32). * Reprinted from *Group Processes: an Introduction to Group Dynamics* by Joseph Luft, by permission of Mayfield Publishing Company. Copyright © 1970 by Joseph Luft.

Objective

The objective of this activity is to enable better self-awareness through an experiential understanding of the Johari Window. By tying the experience to the Scripture, it helps us understand the importance of Christians knowing more about themselves.

Materials Needed

Small paper sacks (one for each person), old magazines, glue or tape, scissors, construction paper, yarn or string.

Time Needed

About one hour. Flexibility is provided by the amount of sharing time at the end.

Instructions

1. The design is introduced using the Scripture pas- **99**

	Known to Self	**Not Known to Self**
Known to Others	**I. ARENA** *(The Public Self)*	**II. BLINDSPOT** *(Inhibiting Interpersonal Relations)*
Not Known to Others	**III. FACADE OR HIDDEN AREA** *(Private Self)*	**IV. AREA OF UNKNOWN ACTIVITY**

Below: The diagrams show the effects of exposure and feedback.
With conditions of exposure:

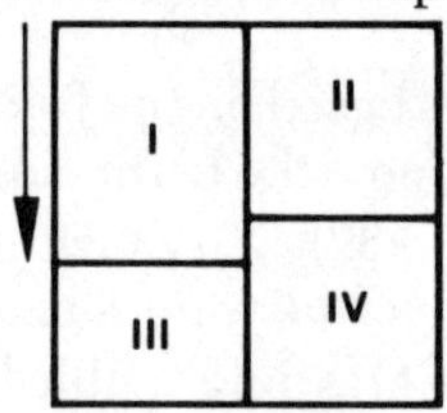

With conditions of feedback:

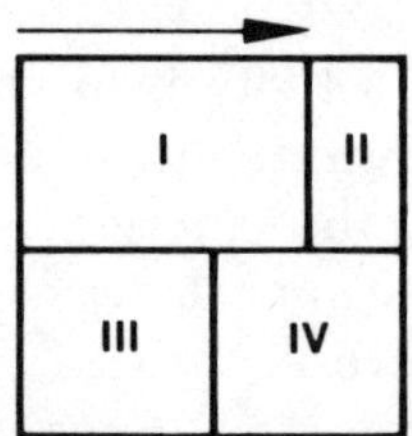

With conditions of exposure and feedback:

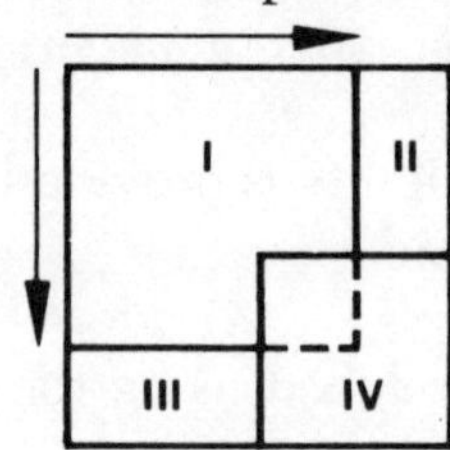

sage. When we talk about the truth in this passage, we are not talking about a lot of "how to's" or theological proofs or religious facts. We are talking about who we, individually, are as persons. The truth about ourselves is the truth that can free us to become what God has for us to be. The leader can model this to the appropriate level for the group.

2. How do we learn more about ourselves? One good way is the Johari Window. Developed by Joe Luft and Harry Ingham (hence the name Johari) the window gives us a good insight into ourselves. It also shows how self-disclosure and feedback from others are valuable in learning and knowing the truth about ourselves.

From the window, we can see areas of ourselves which:

- We know and are willing to tell others.
- We know but choose not to tell others.
- Others know but we do not know.
- Are unknown to either ourselves or others.

Through self-disclosure (telling others more of what I know about me, but they don't know) and feedback (others telling me things I don't know about me), we can make the unknown "pane" of the window smaller. That's another way of saying we know more of the truth about ourselves.

3. How to experience this theory:

- Give everyone a paper sack.
- Have each person make a "necklace" using the yarn and a piece of construction paper. The paper should be worn on the person's back so he or she cannot see it.
- Using the old magazines, have each person cut out pictures, words, or phrases that symbolize those things which are known to self and which you are willing to share with others. Paste or tape these on the outside of the paper sack.

- Place inside the sack those things known to yourself but which you are not willing to share with everyone.
- Find a symbol that represents an *affirmation* you want to give to the other people. These should be genuine and each should be selected especially for the person to whom it is given. Tape or paste it on the construction paper on that person's back.
- Allow about twenty minutes for this part of the exercise. Then call time. Ask that this twenty minutes be done in silence.

To share the experience, ask each person to get with one other person and talk about:

- The meaning of the symbols on the outside of their sacks.
- If they are comfortable in doing it, share something from the inside of the sack (be sure to emphasize that this is optional—they don't have to do it).
- Look at the affirmations received (on the construction paper). Share any feelings resulting from these affirmations.
- Bring everyone back into the total group. If anyone did not understand one of their affirmations, have them request clarification from the person giving it.
4. Summarize by tying the experience back to the window:
- The symbols on the outside of the bag are "public self."
- The symbols on the inside are the "private self."
- The affirmations are the "blind area."
- By sharing (self-disclosure) from the "private self" and receiving (feedback) affirmations in the "blind area" we have reduced the unknown area. By doing that, we have learned more about ourselves and the gifts we possess.

Note: This design should be used only after a group has completed some history giving exercises. It will not work well for a group which is just beginning.

Nonverbal Design

Objective

The objective of this design is to experiment with some forms of communication other than verbal.

Materials Needed

Record player, records.

Time Needed

About one hour.

Instructions

1. The first activity is a game of charades. Before the meeting, the leader needs to write on slips of paper the names of Bible places, people, and events. At least one slip is needed for each person in the group. To start the game, divide the group into two teams. Ask one person on each team to act as timer for the game. To start, ask one person from one of the teams to take a slip, read it, and take a minute to decide how he or she can act out nonverbally to the others on the team the name on the slip. They then have to guess from his actions and movements what the name is. At the end of the minute, give the go signal. Record the amount of time it takes the team to guess the name. Continue the charades until everyone has a turn. Alternate on each turn between the two teams.

This activity promotes team building. It also encourages freedom in nonverbal expression. It gets the group used to role-playing type exercises.

2. The second activity is called "swinging statues" and is based on the old childhood game of the same name. The leader selects one person from the group to be the "statue." The leader then twirls that person around and **103**

around and after several turns lets go. The person has to "freeze" in whatever position he ends up in. Then have the other group members suggest names for the "statue." Take each member in turn and repeat until everyone has been the statue at least once.

This exercise helps people translate words into symbols by representing words and thoughts with body positions.

3. Hand dance—For this exercise, ask everyone to lie down on the floor in a circle with feet pointing in to the center. Play two or three selections of music, each one with a different beat and style. Ask each person to hold his arms up and let their arms "dance" to the music.

This activity encourages free expression of movement in a nonthreatening way. It's also lots of fun.

4. We now want to combine all of these into a nonverbal worship experience. In designing the worship, you can be as creative as you wish. The examples which follow are ones that we used and which worked well. First divide the group into three subgroups. Give them about ten minutes to prepare their part of the worship after the instructions have been given.

● Call to worship—For this part we want to create a statement of worship using symbols in a variety of ways. Props can be used. Or you can draw a rebus puzzle or some other kind of drawing on a large piece of paper. You can use your bodies to spell out letters, something like "faith, hope, and love: and the greatest of these is love."

● Proclamation of the Word—Ask another third of the group to take this one. Nonverbally role playing a passage of Scripture is ideal for this. It's sort of like the charades. One we used was enacting the battle of Jericho. The two men in the group sat on the ground, back to back, staring straight ahead (representing the fortress). Then one of the children led all of the other group members in a march around the fortress in "follow the leader" fashion. They marched around seven times and then made a bugle sound. At that the two men fell over (the walls came tumbling down). Though only the third who planned this part knew what the passage was, all knew after the walls fell.

• Celebration—To complete the worship experience, the final third of the group prepared creative movement and dance to one of the records. Again, they invited the entire group to dance.

5. To complete the event, everyone was asked to sit down in a circle for a closing prayer. The leader started by comparing his closed fist to the way we often are toward others, ourselves, and God. Each person was given a chance to say a one word verbalization of his or her own feelings about the closed fist. This was repeated for the open hand. Then each person was asked to take the hand of the persons on either side, and to offer a one word prayer about the feeling of being in community with others. A song closed the prayer. The prayer was done with eyes open, looking at our hands and at each other.

Sister Sylvia's Sensuous Saturday

Objective
    The objective of this evening was to experience the downtown area of Houston with all of our senses—sound, sight, touch, smell, taste.
Materials Needed
    None.
Time
    Two to three hours.
Instructions
    1. We first gathered at Sylvia's apartment. Everyone was asked to bring something that either smelled good, felt good, looked good, sounded good, or tasted good. We

105

wound up with a guitar that sounded good, fruit and brownies that surely tasted good, a rabbit fur that felt super, and other assorted and unusual objects. We knew that Mende really trusted the group that night when she brought her blanket and allowed everyone in the group to hold it and feel it.

2. After everyone was finished, we drove to a large fountain in the downtown area of Houston. It was after dark, and as everyone gathered, we talked about the sound of the water, and unusual light patterns from the underwater bulbs, even the smell of the water in the air. We thought about wading, but figured that the city fathers might not approve.

3. From there, we moved to the outside elevator at a large downtown hotel. Up we went, experiencing both the sights of being high in the air, and also the sensations of going up and down. As Mende said it, "My tummy feels funny." Then we got out on one of the upper floors and looked down into the hotel lobby, some thirty floors below us. That was a bit spooky.

4. After the hotel, we toured the underground tunnels below the streets of Houston. The walls along the tunnels and shops are made of a variety of material from carpeting to mirrors to tile. We touched each and talked about how different they felt. We could also hear lots of echoes along the almost deserted tunnels. Someone suggested we play leapfrog, and off we went. That bank guard sure gave us a curious look.

5. Back up on the street level, we walked along, sensing such ordinary but unusual sights and sounds as stop lights, cars going by, sirens, night hawks, insects. Mende found a manhole cover quite interesting. She also discovered a tiny wild flower in a crack in the sidewalk. I wonder how many of the thousands who walked that street during the workday are ever aware of such treasures right at their

feet.

6. By now everyone was feeling a bit hungry, so we went to an outdoor German restaurant which featured a small band playing polkas. It was a great way to complete the evening. We danced and ate and sang, and all went home exhausted but renewed.

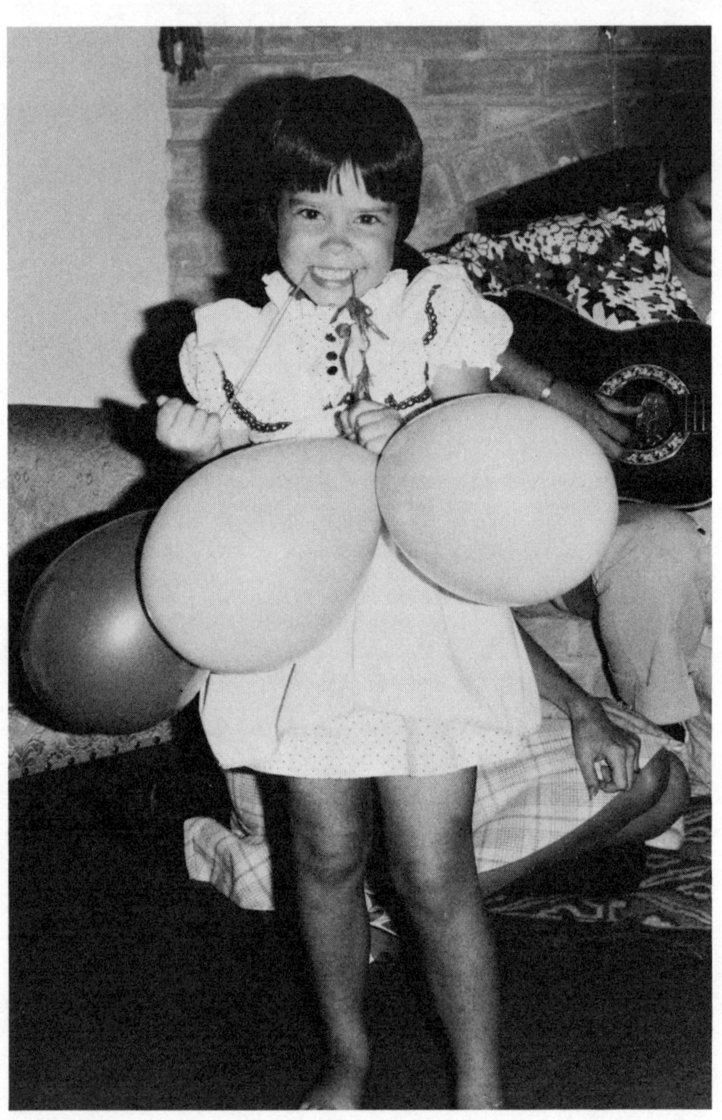

Come to the party!

11

It Works in All Kinds of Places

Almost all of what we have said so far is about a continuing group. It will work equally well in other situations. You may want to try an intergenerational experience at a church family night supper. Or you may want to plan a weekend family conference or retreat. You may want to experiment with an intergenerational Sunday School class. In our own church, our Christian Education Committee decided two summers ago to plan a series of evening celebrations involving the entire church family instead of the traditional Vacation Bible School. It worked quite well.

In any activity involving all ages, the same basic considerations described in previous chapters are important. The objective of a given program will affect how it is designed, but the process is the same.

Let's take another look at the key points to remember:

● Determine the needs and wants of the group for whom you're planning, and design to meet those needs.

● Design your program to be experiential rather than lecture.

● For a one time event or even a series in which the attendance will vary, you won't be able to get much beyond the history giving level. There simply isn't enough time to go beyond that.

• Keep your program activities fast moving. Younger children have a short attention span, and they need lots of variety to hold their interest. Design it to flow smoothly.

• Remember that the younger children will sometimes interrupt. Try to help your audience be comfortable with that. If you are going to work with fifty or more people, you may want to consider having nursery care for those children below five years old. (The larger the group the harder it is for young children to be attentive.)

• Use lots of publicity. Tell people what to expect. If they come expecting a sermon and you ask them to move into discussion groups, some may walk out.

• You probably will have some at the event who have not been in any kind of group situation previously. Keep your activities nonthreatening and reassuring for those who may be a bit nervous.

Keeping these in mind, let's look at the one night event, such as a family night supper or similar event. We call each of these designs a celebration. Each one is an independent program and can therefore be used either by itself or as a series. The objective of each one is to enable all generations participating to have an experience of growth in relationships together.

In planning these events, several considerations are common to all. They are:

• In our planning, we want to ensure that no one in the congregation feels excluded. That is the main reason for calling these "celebrations" rather than "family night" events. For many singles and older couples, a feeling exists that "family" events do not include them. Because a church is a family of Christ, everyone should be included. Stress this in your publicity.

• To set up the discussion groups or "family units"

for each celebration, we use two methods. One way is to ask a natural family (mother, father, children) to "adopt" additional members to create extended families for that one evening. In this way we are able to integrate the single adults and "parentless" youth (youth whose parents are not there) into groups. A second way is to ask a childless couple to adopt children (youth and single adults) to create the extended family. If we are doing a series of celebrations over several nights, we do not try to keep the same groups for each one. Usually attendance varies at these events and it is difficult to maintain continuity. Also, by creating new families at each one, we provide more opportunities for people to get acquainted.

• We like to start each celebration with some singing. This seems to effectively bring everyone together. It provides a time of transition from the day's activities and concerns into the evening program. This "focusing-in" time helps get things started on a positive note. It also gives a bit of time for any late arrivals to get situated before moving into the program. When possible, choose songs that reflect the theme of the evening program. Contemporary or folk religious music with guitar or piano accompaniment is good. Use whatever you are comfortable with.

• With children participating, remind the adults to actively listen to children's answers. Adults may need to ask "how" and "why" to help the children express their feelings.

• One surefire way to get people to turn out for these events is to provide some kind of food or refreshments. This appeals to everyone, brings people together, and provides time for informal fellowship.

• Name tags should be provided at each event. You can use simple stick-on tags, or you can make name tag preparation part of the program. We suggest several different approaches in the designs which you may want to try.

Many of the designs which follow grew out of planning sessions of our Christian Education Committee at the church. That was a fun and exciting process to be part of, and we found that it was another affirmation of the value of group planning and dreaming. Everyone contributed ideas and refinements, and it was a highly creative time. If these designs do not exactly fit your needs, use them as a starting place for developing your own.

We are including the following designs:
1. Celebrate Freedom
2. Celebrate Community
3. Celebrate Growth
4. Celebrate Self
5. Celebrate Christ
6. Noah
7. Sacrifices in the Old and New Testaments
8. Come to the Party

CELEBRATION NO. 1

Celebrate Freedom

The first celebration was held during the 4th of July week and was designed to focus on this event; hence the name Celebrate Freedom.

As people arrived, they were asked to prepare a name tag. For this event, we used simple stick-on name tags. Then they were directed into extended family units and asked to go through three learning centers. We used the "adoption method" where necessary to handle singles and youth whose parents were not there. Family sizes were about ten to twelve people. Once formed, we asked the families to stay together throughout the evening's activities.

Learning Center No. 1

Each family was asked to make a collage on a large white star, cut from poster board. Magazines, scissors, glue, etc. were available on tables for each family to work on. The collage was to express in some way what "family" meant to each group. A poster of instructions was hung in an easy to observe place. Also on the poster were questions designed to enable people to think about the different meanings of the word "family." For example, it can mean the family of man, the family of Christ, a natural family (parents and children), or an extended family. The Scripture used was Ephesians 3:14–20.

Learning Center No. 2

At the second learning center, long strips of red paper were laid out on the floor. Each family was to list or illustrate on the paper petitions or things from which they wanted to be free. The instructions were on a large poster, and gave each person the freedom to express their thoughts in their own way. Examples: a drawing, a picture, a single word, a phrase, a paragraph. Each person could add as many things as desired. Crayons and magic markers were available for writing or drawing on the paper. Also on the instruction poster was a Scripture reference for each family to read and talk about as they worked. The Scripture used was Romans 3:21–26.

Learning Center No. 3

At the third learning center, long strips of white paper were laid out on the floor. Each family was asked to express on the paper in some way (similar to Learning Center No. 2) the freedoms they felt thankful for. Again, **113** each person could add as many as desired. The Scripture suggested for this learning center was 2 Corinthians 4:15.

When all of the stars had been completed, they were placed on a large sheet of blue paper on the floor, forming the star field to an American flag. Then the red and white strips of paper were added to complete the flag. (For this design, the flag can be any convenient size, but should be large enough that people have plenty of room to work.) Our completed flag was about 10 feet × 15 feet. An American flag and a Christian flag on stands were then placed at the corners of the "family" flag.

While the flag was being assembled on the floor, those not involved in working on the assembling task were provided a teaching type of input on the relation of church and state in the United States. Emphasis was placed on the role the church and churchmen played in the forming of our nation. The history of the church in America can be given by either a minister or a lay person. It should last from five to ten minutes. Because of the smaller children, it should not last longer than that. When the large flag had been completed, the families were asked to sit on the floor around it. Then several songs were sung, each related to the theme of freedom.

A closing prayer was used to complete the celebration. Each family was asked to voice, using single words or phrases, prayers of thanksgiving from what they had written on the white stripes. Then, they were asked to voice whatever requests for forgiveness or growth (from the stripe containing their things they wanted to be free from). Finally, everyone was asked to take the hand of the person next to them to form a human bond around the flag. A closing prayer was voiced by the leader.

Following the closing worship experience, homemade ice cream and cookies were served for a time of informal
114 fellowship.

Helpful Hint: To determine the size of the flag needed, estimate the number of people you expect to attend. This particular one at our church was attended by between 150 and 175 people, and we used a flag size of 10 × 15 feet. Adjust your flag size upward or downward depending on the number you expect.

CELEBRATION NO. 2

Celebrate Community

The second celebration was designed to focus on the community of Christ, the family of Christ.

As people arrived, they were asked to prepare name tags. The tags were to be made out of construction paper of various colors. For this celebration, we needed to control the number in groups, so the number of pieces of each color of paper was limited (12). We asked the family units to all use the same color. As people finished their name tags, they came on into the room for group singing. After several songs, groups were formed (according to colors).

Since a number of the people attending had no previous group experience, we wanted to start the sharing time with easy, nonthreatening questions. We used favorite questions: What was your favorite toy as a child? What is your favorite food? What is your favorite time of day? Why?

If the group had already used these questions in some previous exercise, or if they finished quickly, they were asked to go to the "Quaker set."

Physical Warmth Question: Think back to your childhood. Imagine that it's a cold, drizzly day. You are coming in from school, and you are really feeling chilled to the bone, perhaps wet. Where in your

115

home did you go to warm up? How was the home heated?

Spiritual, Emotional Question: In the same way, think about those times when you were feeling down, depressed, your feelings were hurt. Where did you go for comfort, consolation, healing? What or who was your place of spiritual warmth?

On these questions, we asked adults to respond for when they were children. We asked children to respond for the present. Each question was personally modeled by the leaders.

Next, each family was asked to prepare and share a community salad. In the publicity prior to the event, each person was asked to bring one piece of fruit with which to make a fruit salad. The planning committee provided watermelon halves to use as salad bowls. As each group started into the salad making, we asked them to be aware of the feel and smell of each fruit. We also asked them to examine each type of seed from the fruit, thinking about seeds and God's plan for continuing life. All members in each group participated in preparing the salad. When each group had its salad ready to eat, we asked them to offer thanks in some way which they chose (song, prayer, etc.).

While the salads were being eaten, a relational type Bible study was presented for discussion. We used the passage on the wedding at Cana (John 2:1–11). After reading it from the Bible (rhythm story could be used), the leader emphasized that this was a joyous, family celebration and the significance of the fact that Jesus used such an occasion to perform one of his first public miracles. We talked about the good news that Jesus meets our needs today both in quantity and quality, just as he did at the wedding feast. Then, each group was asked to: Describe a situation in your family life in which you felt a special joy of community. Describe a particular joy or sense of community in your life with Christ.

After the meal, all family members joined in the cleanup. Then each family was asked to close the celebration in a way of their own choosing (song, prayer, etc.).

THE WEDDING AT CANA

One bright day in old Nazareth
Jesus decided he had hammered enough
He put away his tools with a joyful heart
He knew his ministry was about to start.
Back from the river after seeing Big John
And a trip to the desert ready to get it on.
He was off to Cana for a wedding feast
But in the middle it had to cease.
Just when the party was boogie'n on,
The servant said "The wine is gone."
Mary said "Son, what can you do?"
Aw gee, Mom, don't tell me what to do.
He told the servants "Go get some jugs
Fill them with water and strain out the bugs."
They filled them with care and filled them fine,
And the next thing you know they had wine.
Not just wine—but the very best wine.
The moral of this story for one and all
Jesus meets our needs both big and small.
Hooray!

Mark and Mary Frances Henry

CELEBRATION NO. 3

Celebrate Growth

The third celebration was designed to focus on ecology and our need to live in relationship with the natural world around us.

To start the evening, each family was asked to bring a picnic lunch. These were eaten together outside on the lawn of the church.

Following the picnic some of the adults took all of the preschool age children and planted flowers in a prepared bed outside the new fellowship hall. At the same time, the other adults worked together to trim and clean the church grounds. At the same time, the senior high youth (with junior highs helping) worked with the elementary aged children to prepare a skit based on the parable of the sower (Luke 8:4–8).

At the designated time, all groups came back together in the fellowship hall for singing. "Joy Is Like the Rain" is a good song for this celebration. The elementary age children then presented their skit. A relational Bible study was used for group discussion. The evening was closed with a liturgy designed for the celebration.

The skit used by the elementary children was taken from the book *Even a Worm* by Elizabeth Blandford. It is published by World Library Publications Inc. The particular celebration used was "Everybody's Got to Grow," and appears on pages 8–10.

The relational Bible story is based on the parable of the sower. The first step is to divide the total group into smaller groups for discussion. A group size of eight to twelve is suggested, divided as evenly in each group between adults and children as possible. It isn't necessary for "natural" families to stay in the same group together, though it is desirable. Younger children are often more comfortable with their parents, while older youth may prefer to be in a group with adults other than their parents. This can go either way, and the decision on whether to keep "natural" families together will depend on the objectives of the celebration. With everyone in a discussion group, the following questions can be used to enable sharing. In using these, the adults should answer for when they were children, and the children should answer for now.

1(a). Thinking back to your childhood, say ages six to twelve, try to remember the first time you planted flowers or seeds, or if you cannot remember anything there, how about a birth (brother, sister, or pet). Describe the event and your feelings as you remember them.

1(b). When you were a child, what did you most like to do on a rainy day, on a stormy day with lots of lightning and thunder? (Use only if it is raining.)

2. Can you remember a particular person (parent, Sunday School teacher, school teacher, relative, friend) who in your childhood or teen years planted the seed of faith in your life? Can you remember how they did this? What was it about that person which made you want to listen and hear what they were saying?

3. Can you think of those areas in your life today which are hard ground? Shallow soil with rock just below the surface? Thistle or weed patches? Fertile soil? Share these with the others in your group.

4. What do you personally hear in this parable that is good news to you right now?

Normally, in doing relational Bible stories, the Scripture is read and then the group questions are asked. For this celebration, we suggest that the children's skit be used in lieu of reading the Bible. Then go into the questions.

After completing the above questions, each group can close with a prayer or song or some other appropriate way of celebrating their time and sharing.

To bring the total group back together and close the evening, a special prayer can be used. It is found in the book *Even a Worm* and appears on pages 8 and 9. The **119** prayer was written to go with the skit and the parable.

In addition to the book, other required material for this celebration include flowers to be planted, gardening tools, trash bags, and any other needed yard tools, depending on the extent of the clean-up activity planned. In case of rain, the event can be moved inside with minor changes. Obviously, the flower planting and the clean-up cannot be done. Window washing, painting, or other touch-up repairs on the inside of the church buildings can be substituted. A story time or movie or other special design can be substituted for the preschoolers. The picnic can be held in the fellowship hall. The other activities can go on unchanged.

To work with the rain problem, special activities can be planned. If the rain is not severe, and the temperature is warm enough, an activity can be done to focus attention on the rain and its analogy to our Christian faith. For example, the preschoolers could be taken out in the rain for a brief moment to experience the feel, sound, and sight of falling rain. Here the leaders would have to focus their (the children's) attention on these things. Obviously, you do not do this in a real downpour or a thunderstorm, although in this case you could go out on a covered porch or to a large window and still do the exercise. The importance of rain in nature could be discussed. Rain has a cleansing effect, and after a rain notice how everything looks cleaner and greener outside. This can also be used as an analogy of God's forgiveness. Wind can be used as an analogy to God in the sense that wind is real, we can feel it, we can see its effects, but we cannot actually see the wind. The same is true for God. The importance and the need for rain to enable growth in the natural world is like God's love being necessary for our growth as persons. Just as the rain soaks into the ground

120 and disappears in order to feed plants, God's love soaks into us and helps us to grow. Just as the weather can be turbulent, with wind, lightning, the thunder, so can life be turbulent. Yet out of the storm can come growth, both in nature and in people. These are a few ideas that can be used to take advantage of a rainy day, rather than to let it spoil the celebration. Also, though these events and activities have been described for the preschoolers, they can be used for all ages, including adults.

CELEBRATION NO. 4

Celebrate Self

The purpose of the fourth celebration was to focus on our personhood and celebrate the unique person God has made each of us to be. This celebration combined a potluck supper with learning center activities.

Each family was asked to bring a dish (usual potluck meal procedure). While the meal is being set up, people are asked to go to each learning center. Each center has a poster of instructions.

Learning Center No. 1

Each person was asked to make a large name tag. Construction paper, yarn, felt-tip pens, scissors, etc. were available. The instructions were: make a name tag that tells others something about you. Attach it to a piece of yarn and wear it around your neck for the evening. Throughout the evening share informally with others what the tag says about you.

Along with the instructions on the poster was the following statement: "The most painful thing and the most beautiful thing about me is my name. Painful because it sets me apart; beautiful because it says 'I am.' "

Learning Center No. 2

Along one wall of the room was a giant calendar. Each month was a separate poster board. Each day was about three to four inches square. Under the calendar on a table were assorted stick-ons, paper, scissors, glue, crayons, etc. Each person was asked to find his or her birth date and decorate that square with the materials provided. We also asked (on the instructions) that people leave some room in "their" block in case someone else had the same birth date. In that case, we also asked these people to meet each other and celebrate the serendipity of their same birthday.

Learning Center No. 3

This center provided the basis for group discussion following supper. It was designed to enable each person to explore the meaning of their own name. On a couple of tables, we had several copies of the paperback book *4000 Names for Your Baby* (Dell Publishing, 1974) containing the meanings of names. We asked each person to look up his or her name and write the meaning on an index card.

As each person completed their learning center activity, they went through the food line. We encouraged families to sit together for the meal, but did not insist on it.

Following the meal (as the tables were being cleared) we sang several songs. "Do You Know Who You Are?" "God Has Called You," and "I Heard the Lord Call My Name" were songs that we used.

Then we moved into family groups. Each individual in the group was asked to share with each other the meaning of his name, history of the name (i.e., named for someone special), and how well he felt his name fit him. Next, the leaders talked about God calling each of us by name, using the biblical examples of Samuel, Moses, and Paul. Focusing on how these men responded to God's call, the groups were asked: If God called you by name today, right now, how would you respond? What in your life would keep you from answering God's call?

Finally the leader talked about how in the Bible God changed names: Abram to Abraham, Simon to Peter, Saul to Paul. Then we asked them to share their answers to: How would each person change his or her name if given the opportunity? Why? How did they feel God would change their name; or how would each person want God to change his or her name?

For closing, each group was asked to close either in prayer or in whatever way they felt led to close.

CELEBRATION NO. 5

Celebrate Christ

This celebration was designed to focus on Christ and in particular on the family of Christ. After several opening songs, we divided into groups for a Bible study. For the first one, we asked each group to select a passage of Scripture dealing with Christ's ministry and to develop it into a pantomime, involving all members of the group. Then we asked each group to present their's to the other groups, asking the others to guess what passage they were seeing.

For the second study, we focused on the passage in 1 Corinthians 12:12–31. After reading the passage, we asked each group to answer the following:

• What is something that I do well that contributes to the body of Christ. (As part of this question, you may also want to have others in the group affirm that person by adding other things they know of that the person does well.)

● What does it take to run a church like the one you are in? What kinds of jobs are there? What would happen if everyone tried to be the pastor, or the church secretary, or a church officer?

● What are some of the ways we celebrate being a part of the body of Christ?

One of the ways we can celebrate is the *agape* feast, and this is used to close the evening. The leader should describe to the group what *agape* is. Historically it comes out of Middle Eastern culture and the Passover meal of Judaism. Christ was celebrating the Passover meal, or *agape*, with his disciples in the upper room, and from it he went on to establish the sacrament of the Lord's Supper. From the customs of those days we get the idea of seating everyone on the floor around a table. A large white table cloth (a white king-size sheet will handle about forty people) can be spread on the floor to symbolize this. Everyone sits around it. You can also have each group at its own "table" if you prefer. For the *agape* meal, you can use loaves of bread (have some members of your church bake them). If you want to go a bit farther with the symbolism, try other foods from the Bible: dried fruit, figs, olives, cheese. We suggest using an *agape* rather than Communion because in most denominations, younger children are not permitted to participate in Communion until after joining the church as communing members. This restriction does not apply with the *agape*. It is important to explain the difference of the two.

After sharing the meal, close the evening with a prayer and/or an appropriate song.

CELEBRATION NO. 6

Noah

124   The time allotted for this session is one and one-half

hours. Focus is around the story of Noah and his family.

At the name tag learning center, the following materials should be provided: colored construction paper (eight sheets of each color), magazines containing animal pictures which can be torn out and pasted to the name tag if desired, crayons and/or magic markers, scissors, and glue. Yarn should be provided to tie the name tag around necks to make a necklace. The instructions are:

1. Select a color paper you particularly like.
2. Tear or cut it into the shape of an animal—one that you for some reason identify with.
3. Decorate the name tag with pictures, drawings, however you want to. Make a real creation that says something about you and where you are as a person.
4. When you have completed the name tag, wear it around your neck for the rest of the evening. As time permits, share with others in the group what your name tag means and why you made it the way you did.

Ice Breakers—The first activity of the evening will be ice breakers. The purpose of these is to get people to loosen up and to begin to set aside the concerns and thoughts of the day in order to focus on the events and activities of the evening.

Family Questionnaire—This questionnaire is designed to enable people to get to know each other quickly, have some fun, and get things started off on a light note. Give everyone a copy of the questionnaire, follow the instructions given, and see who can complete it first. For the smaller children, their parents may need to help them. A copy of the questionnaire is included in Chapter 12.

Singing—Sing a couple of fun songs that follow the theme of the evening. (Two examples are "Rise and Shine," and "The Butterfly Song.")

The next activity is to get people into groups of six to eight. This can be done on the basis of the color of their name tags. With each color limited to about eight sheets of paper, there should be seven or eight people with the same color. At the point of forming the groups, the leader will instruct everyone to find others who have the same color name tag they do and to form a group. For those younger children who may be uncomfortable with someone other than their own parents, they may stay with them. After the groups are formed and seated in group circles, move on to the next activity.

Rhythm story of Noah—This is a specially designed version of the story of Noah. Its purpose is to focus the entire group's attention on the story to provide the base for the following activities.

The purpose of the next exercise is to enable each group to become a team by participating together in a fun, joint activity. To get started, give each group a two- or three-inch stack of old newspapers and a roll of masking tape. Instruct them to use these materials to construct a boat. Make sure everyone in the group participates. The boat must be large enough for the smallest member of the group to get into. It can be a raft, a houseboat, a rowboat, a sailboat, or whatever the group wants to make. After all are completed, demonstrate them to the entire group. Allow about fifteen minutes for the construction effort. After everyone has looked at all of the boats, ask them to return to their groups and to debrief with the following questions:

● Talk about how the group worked together. Who did the planning? How was the planning done? How about the design? Who took charge and directed the group? How were the tasks divided? Did everyone participate?

● Conclude by explaining that Noah and his family were faced with many of these same questions and decisions.

If you do not have fifteen minutes in the total schedule, a faster alternative is to use the human machine exercise from Lyman Coleman's book *Breaking Free*. If you choose to use this exercise, alter the instructions slightly to say that the machine must represent some piece of equipment that would be required to live on an ark for a year.

History Giving—This activity is designed to enable the members of each group to get to know each other on a common ground. To set up for the exercise, each group needs to be in a "double wagon wheel," in which half of the group is in an outward facing circle and the other half is opposite them in an inward facing circle. They may be either seated or standing. The leader will ask a question which the partners (the people facing each other in the two circles) are to answer. After allowing time for each to answer, the leader will instruct the outer circle to rotate one person to the right. Then she will ask the next question, repeating the process until the people in the two circles are back facing their original partners. The questions to be asked are:

What was your favorite pet as a child and why?

What was your favorite hiding place as a child and why?

(On this question, try to imagine if such a place would exist on the ark.) What is your favorite time of day and why? What was the first long trip you can remember taking as a child?

What was the mode of transportation used on that trip?

Can you remember how you felt about it? If you can take a trip now to anyplace in the world, and money were no problem, where would you go and why? Who would you like to take with you on that trip, other than immediate family, Why?

Relational Bible Study—The biblical story of Noah will **127** be read. Then the leader will guide the groups into a relational study of the story. Each person will be asked to share their answers to the following: Who in this story do you most closely identify with and why? Noah, his sons, the wives, the children, the neighbors, the people of the world. Assume you are one of Noah's family, what would be your reaction if Grandpa Noah came in one day and said, "I've been talking to God. We're going to build a boat, a very big boat." Remember that you live in a desert-like area with no large body of water around for miles. Would you think Noah had lost his marbles? Would you humor him? Would you tend to ignore him? Try to imagine how you would react if your dad or grandpa came in and made a statement like that today. As you think about this story, try to identify the "good news" for you personally. What is God saying to you through this story. Have a little fun with the story, and see if the group can come up with a new name for the story—The great flood; Grandpa knows best; etc.

Affirmation Exercise—This exercise enables people to begin to say good things to each other, affirm each other. In the groups, ask each person in turn to sit quietly while the others in the group affirm her or him. The affirmation statement is "I see you as a (certain animal) and why." Example, "I see you as a collie dog because you're always so friendly and happy and I just feel good when I'm around you because of your cheerful personality."

Closing Time—To close the evening experience, have each group close together in prayer. Ask each person in turn to state his or her needs for a specific prayer (a need, a concern, a fear, a joy, a thanks). Then ask the group to pray with that person about that thing. Then go on to the next person. The purpose of this is to encourage people to pray out loud, to enable people to pray for and with each other. After all people in each group have completed their "turn," the group may want to close by standing and holding hands, singing or praying a closing prayer together.

A time of informal fellowship can follow if the total group desires. Try animal crackers for a dessert.

Noah

(Leader starts rhythm by slapping knees. Maintaining the rhythm, she reads the first line. Group repeats each line, in turn, after the leader.

Use this approach in all rhythm stories.)

One bleak Monday many years back
The world was wicked, the world was black.
Folks down there were really bad
All their sinnin' made God very sad.

He was sorry he had made it,
It broke his heart.
So he said to himself
I'll make a fresh start.

There was *one* man who was really good
He always did what God said he should.
With his three fine sons and all their wives
They'd been good all their lives.

Meanwhile, the crime rate was a risin'
The people were a jivin'.
The world was rotten to the core.
And the Lord said,
    Looking bad,
    Looking sad,
    I'm gettin' mad!
So the Lord said to Noah,

Go build a boat.
A real big boat.
A mighty big boat.
Do exactly what I say,
And you'll be OK.
Old Noah and his sons began to build
With hammer and saw they became quite skilled
The neighbors threw a party just to laugh,
And Noah said,

      How long can you tread water?
When the boat was completed they christened its bow,
And quickly gathered a zebra, a pig and a cow;
Kangaroos and chim-pan-zees,
Dogs and cats and too many fleas.
A large hippopotamus, a little tiny mouse,
All those animals stuffed that house.

The ark was ready
The ark was closed
The sky grew dark,
And the thunder rolled.

It rained and it poured
and the wind blew cold
WOOOOOOOOOOOOOOOOOOOOO
and on the ark they all grew bored.

Forty days and forty nights
No TV
No monopoly
and no CB.

God didn't forget about Noah and the boat
He made very sure they stayed afloat.
A long time later the world dried out
130 The world was clean, and God gave a shout

The ark came to rest on Ararat
Great, jumpin' Jehosaphat!

God said
Get out of that boat
You wanta' spend your life afloat?

They all came out, they all moved on
They walked into a bright new dawn.

MARK AND MARY FRANCES HENRY

CELEBRATION NO. 7

Sacrifices in the Old and New Testaments

This celebration focuses on the offering of sacrifices in the old Testament and contrasts that with Jesus becoming the sacrifice for all people.

To form groups, use the names of the twelve tribes of Israel. On a table near the entry, place twelve sets of name tags made from construction paper. Each set should contain ten tags of the same color. Write the tribe name on each set. The twelve tribes are Reuben, Simeon, Gad, Judah, Issachar, Zebulun, Ephraim, Manasseh, Benjamin, Dan, Asher, and Naphtali. You may need to combine some tribes if your total group is small. As people arrive, ask them to choose a tribe, put their name on the tag, and wear it for the evening.

Use some singing to get things going. Then move into a relational Bible study of Genesis 22:1–19. For group sharing, ask the following questions:

1. Remembering that Isaac was very precious to his father, Abraham, imagine you are asked by God to

131

give up something that is very dear to you (person, pet, object). How would you feel?

2. In the story, God provided an animal for the sacrifice at the last moment. Centuries later, he provided a sacrifice for all of us in Jesus. Try to imagine how you would feel, as someone who had known Jesus well, seeing him alive three days after you had seen him killed. Would you feel surprise, shock, disbelief, suspicion, joy?

Abraham's trust in God was truly incredible. So was Jesus' as he willingly, knowing full well what was coming, allowed himself to be taken. We don't often think much about that kind of trust and faith. One way to focus on it is to take a trust walk. Ask everyone to move into pairs. (Make sure children pair with an adult.) Ask one partner to close their eyes. Have the other partner lead the "blind" partner around for about five minutes. Then have them switch roles. Each leader should help his partner become aware of his other senses and what they tell him: smell, sound, touch, taste.

At the end of the ten minutes, have everyone gather around "Mt. Moriah." The mountain can be a small hill or some other designated place on the church lawn or parking lot. Ask the partners to share with each other their answers to the following: 1. How did it feel to blindly follow someone, knowing that your safety was in their hands? Were you nervous or frightened? 2. Compare this with your present relationship with Jesus Christ. (For the child below age ten, this question may be difficult. Change the wording to "Would you let Jesus lead you like this? Why?")

Now move everyone back into their tribes. Ask the tribes to gather around the "mountain." (Three tribes to a mountain is about a crowd, so you may want to have several mountains.) Ask each tribe to select two elders (at least one must be an adult). Have the elders prepare a sacrificial fire on each mountain. (You don't need a huge bonfire. Use sand to protect the grass. You'll need to have wood available.)   While the fires are being prepared, give a *brief* teaching to the total group on Hebrews 10:1–25. This passage contrasts the Old Testament sacrifices required by Jewish law to the sacrifice of Christ, which is forever. Note that the same God who provided a sacrifice for Abraham to use in place of Isaac has also provided a sacrifice for each of us.

Now give everyone a slip of paper and a pencil. Give each tribe a large paper sack. Ask everyone to answer the following question on the paper: Write on the paper the one thing that you would ask Christ to remove from your life right now so that you could have a closer relationship with him. These will not be shared with anyone, so be as honest as you wish. Have everyone fold their papers and place them in the sack. Pray silently together. Have the "elders" place the sacks on the fires. Ask everyone to be aware that as the paper burns the writing on it disappears. In the same way, Jesus forgives us when we ask him, and our guilt disappears with his forgiveness.

To celebrate our freedom from sin through Jesus' sacrifice sing a song and dance about the mountain. The song "Lord of the Dance" can be changed in tempo so that hora can be danced to it. If your group isn't comfortable with that, just walk in a circle around the fire singing a song everyone knows.

By now your fire should be about right for roasting marshmallows, so bring on the refreshments and enjoy a time of informal fellowship.

<h1 style="text-align:center">CELEBRATION NO. 8</h1>

<h2 style="text-align:center">Come to the Party</h2>

This celebration was inspired by the "Come to the Party" concept presented by Karl Olsson in his book, *Come to the Party*.

As people arrived they were asked to prepare a name tag. Colored construction paper was used, with enough squares (size 4″ × 6″) of each color to limit group sizes to ten people (adults and children). Balloons, with colors matching the name tag paper, had previously been hung from the ceiling to mark the spot at which each group was to form.

About five minutes before the scheduled starting time, singing was started. Light, fast songs were used, accompanied by guitar. Songs used were: "It's a Happy, Happy Day"; "I'm Gonna Thank Him"; "Come and Go with Me"; "We Really Want to Thank You, Lord."

After the singing, the leaders briefly welcomed everyone to the "party." Points made were: The purpose of the evening is to have an enjoyable experience. In having a good time, we want everyone to experience in a hopefully new way the fun and joy that God's life for us can provide. Next, the groups were asked to share their individual answers to the following question (including the children): What was the most memorable party you can remember as a child? Describe it and tell why you remember it; what made it so memorable?

Following this question, the leaders provided more input on the joy of Christian living. Points made were: When we think of a party, we think of fun, good feelings. Compare that with the feelings of joy and excitement that we can have at God's party. Note that Jesus' first recorded miracle in public was done at a wedding party.

It's OK to enjoy life as a Christian. We don't have to be unhappy and always somber and serious to be a Christian. In Genesis, we are told that God made us and he himself declared "It was good."

Let's set aside the gloomy, doomy unworthies, that part of us which is admittedly bad and sinful (in no way trying to deny that side, but rather to look at the positive side also), at least for this one evening. Let's try to focus on and claim the good side, the joyful part of us.

Next, the parable of the prodigal son was read. However, instead of reading it from the Scripture, a rhythm story version was used. The leaders followed this with an introduction to the concept of God's party, using relational Bible study methods. Points made about the party (following Karl Olsson's book) were:

Using the biblical story, we can think of the Christian life as a party which the father held for his returning son. Call it God's party. Who do you most closely identify with in this story? The prodigal, the older brother, the father, the rich friends of the prodigal, the servants, maybe even the fatted calf?

Using the analogy of the party, our responses to God's invitation can be one of the following: There is no party (Christian life-style). This whole thing is a figment of someone's imagination. There is a party going on, but I'm not invited (I'm not worthy). There's a party, but I can't stay unless I keep working hard (Earning my grace.) There's a party, I'm at it, and I am free to enjoy it and celebrate it.

The groups were then asked to answer the following question. Before telling them to start, the leaders modeled their answers: Where do you see yourself with respect to God's party in your Christian life? Where do you really want to be?

While the groups were processing these questions, **135**

the leaders gave each group a paper bag containing material with which to make party decorations, including: crepe paper, tissue paper, balloons, masking tape, markers, and crayons.

After the groups finished with the questions, they were asked to prepare for a party using the contents of the bag. They were instructed to prepare a banner, decorate each other, decorate the room, whatever their group chose to do. Fifteen minutes were allowed for the group to prepare their decorations.

A song was used to bring the total group back together after they completed their decorations. It is "The Wedding Banquet" and is based on the Scripture in Matt. 22:1–14. Following the singing, each group was asked to describe their decoration and its meaning.

The leaders then talked briefly about the analogy between the room now being ready for a celebration and the world, readied by God for the celebration of life. Like the room all ready for the party, there can be no party until the invited guests celebrate it, coming together. Likewise, there is no party in our world until we can claim and celebrate God's invitation. As in the "Wedding Banquet" song, we can get locked into roles that prevent us from accepting God's invitation. "I have married a wife, bought a cow, have fields, and commitments, etc." We can get so locked into performing the role of husband or wife, job, etc. that we forget all of them are gifts of God's party.

Following the input, the groups were asked: What prevents you from coming to God's party right now?

After answering the question, everyone was asked to stand and move around among the other groups, everyone mingling and inviting each other specifically to God's party. Then a large circle was formed and we sang

 "Lord of the Dance" with everyone dancing to the

Bunny Hop around the room.

After the song, everyone sat down on the floor in a large circle. A Mexican piñata was hanging from the ceiling. Inside, instead of candy, were slips of paper on which a blessing was written (God loves you, Peace, Joy, Shalom, etc.) (The blessings had been prepared by each person when they arrived. Paper, pens, and instructions were located at the name tag table so that people could write or draw a blessing at the same time they made their name tags.) In keeping with tradition, the youngest child was invited to break the piñata. Each successively older child was given a chance until the piñata broke, spilling its blessings on all. Each person received at least one blessing. A large balloon may be used in place of the piñata.

A closing prayer was offered, with everyone in a large huddle. Following the conclusion of the program, everyone moved to the kitchen for fresh, homemade ice cream and cookies. Informal fellowship completed the evening.

12

Family Retreats

Family camps or retreats offer added flexibility in your planning. Usually these are weekend events, so you have more time to work. Depending on the location you may have some physical surroundings you can build into the design. A typical design will look something like this:

- Friday Evening—Registration and getting settled in. Depending on the facility and the time required to travel to it, you may or may not want to include supper. About 8:00 P.M., have a general session. Start with singing. Follow with a brief input, welcoming everyone, stating any rules of the facility, and then setting the theme for the retreat. Then move everyone into their extended family groups for the weekend. Give them a couple of easy history-giving questions and end the program. If possible, some refreshments would be good at this point. Remember to keep the program brief on this first evening, especially if people have had to travel some distance to get there. They'll be tired.

- Saturday Morning—Plan your program time from 9:00 A.M. to 12:00 or 12:30 P.M. In general, we suggest that you use a pattern of input from the leaders, followed by an experiential exercise. An input of fifteen to twenty minutes is plenty. Avoid sermons.

- Saturday Afternoon—Leave it open for free time. Some organized games are OK (volleyball, softball, etc.), but don't plan a program. Families need to have some playtime together, and this is the time.

- Saturday Evening—You can plan a couple of hours of program time here, provided you keep it moving and include variety. If you want to provide input, keep it short and to the point.

- Sunday Morning—We prefer to build around a worship time for Sunday morning. We also like to make the worship a bit different from the traditional church service. Since you are away from the church building at home, you are generally more open to some changes. Try to enable everyone to participate fully in the worship. One very effective way to do this is to ask each group to design and lead a segment of the worship. Encourage each group to role play the Scripture rather than just read it, or some other way. The message can be a nonverbal presentation. You'll be amazed at the unique ideas people come up with when given the encouragement and permission to try.

In planning your program for the weekend, remember that it's a family event. Plan most of the activities so that all ages can interact together. You may want to build in some time for peer groups to be together, but then tie that back into the total process so it enables intergenerational communication. In general, try to avoid the traditional Sunday School pattern of adults with adults, children with children, and teens with teens.

As you work with your theme, try to keep it simple. It's very easy to try to cover too much territory in a weekend. As an example, if your theme is "covenanting" in the family, you might ask families on Sunday morning to develop a convenant for their family. It is tempting to try to redirect a family life-style for the coming year through a broad covenant. That won't work very well. It's much easier to commit to a single change for a month than to a dozen for a year. As families gain some experience and success in a simple covenant, then they can go farther. So, keep your theme simple and straightforward. Beware of making it so philosophical or theological that no one can understand it or deal with it.

To give you an example of how to design a weekend, we've included one which we did for a church weekend retreat. It's based on the Come to the Party idea, and it was a most successful weekend.

To get started in the planning for the retreat, we first spent an entire day with the planning committee from the church. We wanted both them and us to understand their needs as they saw them. We then explained some possible designs to meet the needs they identified. Out of that came preliminary design. Continuing to review and revise with the committee, we arrived at the final plan for the weekend. Here again, we found the value of working with a committee in developing a plan that met their needs. There are a lot of ideas lying around in people's heads waiting for someone to ask for them.

As you read over the design, think about how you might plan a weekend for your group or church.

Weekend Retreat

Letting Yourself Love

Goals
1. Get to know each other better
2. Grow in personal faith
3. Enable "family of Christ" within church
4. Initiate small group activity in church

Blocks of Time
Friday night   9:00 P.M. to 9:45 P.M.
Saturday morning   Breakfast at 8:00 A.M.
                             Program time 9:00 to 11:30 A.M.
                             Lunch at 12:00
Saturday afternoon   Free Time to 3:30
                             Workshops from 3:30 to 5:00
                             Dinner at 6:00
Saturday evening   Program time from 7:00 to 9:00 P. M.
Sunday morning   Breakfast at 8:00 A.M.
                             Program/Worship 9:00 to 11:30
                             (with a break in the middle)

Friday Evening
The purpose is to bring the group together, introduce the weekend, and have a brief time of group activities:

Singing—Open with songs everyone knows. After two or three of these, it will be OK to introduce a new one or two. It is important that these opening songs be light, fast, and easy to sing.

Family Questionnaire—a copy is attached. It is designed to introduce people to each other, have fun doing it, and learn a bit about each other, all in a nonthreatening way.

Relational Bible Study and Response—We used the passage in Mark 10:13–16 in which Jesus talks about coming as a child. The song "Come as a Little Child" by Avary and Marsh fits well here, either as a reading or as a solo. We then closed the evening with a song and a prayer.

Saturday Morning
The purpose is to continue the process of getting to know each other and to introduce the concept of affirma-

tion and its importance to us, both as individuals and as families.

After the opening singing, we moved into groups. (We had not done this on this particular retreat on Friday night because many of the people were late arriving due to a long drive.) To get into groups, we asked each child to find an adult with whom he wanted to be in a group. For those children who were too young to feel comfortable doing this, we asked them to stay with their parents. Once everyone was in pairs (or threes—you may want each child to pick two adults depending on the number of people attending), ask each pair to find another pair. This will get everyone into groups of either four or six.

We did some warm-up exercises, using from Lyman Coleman's books games like the "hot ball toss," the "frog relay," and the "human machine." Then we asked the groups to sit down and share with each other their answers to the following:

- How did you heat your home during the years you were age six to twelve?
- What was your favorite dessert during those years?
- On a rainy summer day, what did you most like to do?
- Who was your hero, your idol?

We took a twenty minute break at this point. With children involved, we've found that a break after a sharing time is a good idea. It gives them a chance to run off a bit of energy after sitting for a bit.

After the break with people back into their groups, we read the IALAC story. You'll find it on page 23 of the March 1974 issue of *Faith at Work* magazine. It is also reprinted at the end of this chapter. As it was being read, we had two adults and two children acting it out. Then we **142** asked the groups to answer the following questions:

- Try to think of the ways you take bites of the IALAC cookies of other members of your family.
- How can you give first aid to a broken IALAC?
- How do you feel when someone won't accept your gift of first aid to them?
- How would you want others in your family to give your IALAC first aid?

This will probably use up the morning time. If you still have a few minutes left over and want to try one more group exercise, add a Bible pantomime here. Have each group select a passage of Scripture, decide how to act it out, using everyone in the group, then perform it for the other groups. See how long it takes them to guess what each group is doing.

Lunch

Free Time—This particular church wanted to have some topic workshops in the late afternoon, so we planned these for the 3:30 to 5:00 P.M. time period. During this time, you'll need to provide some supervision for the younger children while the parents are in the workshops. We suggest that if you do want to use the workshop approach for your weekend, make them optional. Some suggested workshop topics you might want to consider are:

- Self-esteem for elementary group
- Self-esteem for teens
- Mid-life crisis
- Communicating in marriage
- Relational Bible study and conversational prayer
- TA for families
- Small groups in the church
- Value clarification for families

There may be others your group will be interested in. We limited each workshop to forty-five minutes, repeating them so that people could attend two if they wanted.

Saturday Evening

Our objective for Saturday evening was to have a time for fun and fellowship and to continue the group process. After some singing, one of the leaders read the parable of the prodigal son as a rhythm story. A copy of it is attached. This was used as the introduction to a relational Bible study on this passage, using the party concept Karl Olsson talks about in his book, *Come to the Party*. Refer to Celebration 8, Chapter 11.

We followed the study with a real party. Each group was given a party sack containing crepe paper, balloons, material to make banners out of, or party hats—whatever each group wanted to do. Crayons and magic markers, scissors, glue, and construction paper can all be used for this. Time was provided for each group to prepare their part of the party. They could do a skit, sing a song, lead the entire group in something—we gave them complete freedom to dream up whatever they wanted.

And then the party began. It was a real serendipity. The kids and adults played together beautifully. A Vietnamese family being helped by the church was able to fully participate, even though they didn't understand our language at all. That's the beauty of this type of design. You can never predict what is going to happen when people respond with real joy and celebration. It's amazing what can happen when we give ourselves permission to play.

After the celebration, we asked everyone to join together in a large circle for a closing prayer. Everyone was invited to offer their own one word or short phrase prayers. Refreshments were served afterwards (whoever heard of a party without refreshments?).

Sunday Morning

The objective was to celebrate the time together in worship and prepare for the return home. We started the morning in groups by asking each group to prepare a communal doodle (a group exercise from one of Lyman Coleman's books). This takes about thirty minutes. Then we talked a bit about the various parts of a worship service and what each part means. We talked about the prayer, music, call to worship, Scripture reading, sermon, benediction, etc. Each group was then asked to volunteer to plan one part of the service and lead the entire group in that part during the worship service. We gave them about twenty minutes to prepare. After a short break, we began the worship service. Following the worship, we all moved outside under a large oak tree and sat on the grass for an *agape* feast. A closing song and prayer concluded the retreat.

Lunch and Depart for Home

For this retreat, a nursery was provided for the infants and younger children. We brought in even these younger ones for the party on Saturday night and also for the worship on Sunday morning.

FAMILY QUESTIONNAIRE

INSTRUCTIONS: Read the instructions carefully. Do what each one says. Don't skip around—take each item in order. Play fast and fair.

1. Get the signatures of four people you would like to know better after tonight:

______________________   ______________________

______________________   ______________________

2. Get the signatures of two families which are the same size as yours:

______________________   ______________________

3. Find a family with two or more redheads and get their
   name: _______________________________________

4. Find a girl or woman with size seven shoes or a boy or
   man with size ten shoes and write down the number
   of people you asked before one said yes: __________

5. Autographs of four blonds (male or female):

   _________________________   _________________________

   _________________________   _________________________

6. Meet the person closest to you right now: ________

7. Find the girl (if you're a girl, find the boy) with the
   nicest smile and get his or her name: ____________

8. Get the names of two people who have birthdays in
   the same month as yours:

   _________________________   _________________________

9. Autographs of two people (male or female) who cry at
   movies:

   _________________________   _________________________

10. Find someone who mashes the toothpaste in the
    middle: ____________________________________

11. Get the signatures of two people who were born at
    least 1,000 miles from here:

    _________________________   _________________________

12. Find someone who can ice skate: ______________
13. Find someone under age six who can whistle: ______
14. Find a boy under ten with clean fingernails: ______
15. Find a boy under fourteen who doesn't own a
    skateboard: ______________________________

The Care and Feeding of IALACs
by Esther Howard

Most people have never seen or heard of an IALAC,*
yet it is everyone's most precious possession. Each day

*I am indebted to Peter Finck, a school psychiatrist in
Montgomery County, MD., for the symbol of the IALAC.*

our IALAC's grow or get broken off and diminished. We feel happy when they grow and miserable when they are broken. IALAC's, you see, are those deep inside feelings that "I Am Lovable and Capable."

Peter had a dream in which his IALAC became visible. Like a large fragile cookie, it hung around his neck with the words, "I Am Lovable and Capable" all shimmery and alive on it. He wanted everyone to share his exciting discovery.

But while he was getting dressed and wondering if other people's IALAC's would show that day, he heard his mother's voice screaming from downstairs, "Peter, get yourself down here before I come after you." Oops! He felt a piece of his IALAC crumble to the floor.

When he got to breakfast his father was hidden behind his newspaper and didn't notice him until he accidently spilled his milk. It splashed clear across the table and onto his Dad's suit. "You clumsy oaf. Look what you've done," his father barked at him. Peter felt more of his IALAC drop to the floor. He left his breakfast uneaten and went out the front door to look for his best buddy. But on the way to school more pieces broke off when his friend ignored him and the other kids laughed when his lunch sack split and his food went all over the sidewalk. His English teacher said he was a sloppy writer and someone called him a sissy on the playground. His IALAC grew smaller and smaller.

Peter felt so badly after school that he decided he'd tell his mother he was sick. Maybe she'd give him some medicine or something. But she wasn't home when he got there. Instead, there was a note that said, "Take the dinners out of the freezer and turn the oven to 425 degrees. I'll be back at 5:30." By now his IALAC was so small he decided not to go out and play and slumped down instead in front of the TV.

When his parents came home the dinners were out, but he'd forgotten to turn on the oven. So they said he was irresponsible and could never remember anything.

At dinner he felt better when his father asked him about school. But just as he was starting to tell them about the movie he'd seen the phone rang and his father left in the middle of his sentence. When he came back he had something else on his mind. Peter felt his IALAC crumbling all around the edges.

When Peter went to bed that night he lay thinking about the little piece of the "I" that was all he had left. He felt so sad and lonely that he put the pillow over his head so no one could see him suck his thumb. It was a baby thing to do, but the only way he knew to comfort himself for what had happened to his IALAC that day.

Peter wished there was some way to explain it all to his parents so that tomorrow he wouldn't have to watch his IALAC being torn apart all over again. But he fell asleep before he could think of anything.

For all the Peters and Pattys who experience anything like this—as well as their Mommys and Daddys—let's see what answers we can come up with. Let's begin by pretending that we each can see the IALAC's around our necks, hanging there all quivering and alive with feelings, yet so easily damaged by these enemies: Distrust, Disgust, Distance, Disrespect and Discounting.

All of these belong to the same family. You'll see that their family name comes first, and it's *Dis*, which means "taking away from." When Distrust comes along he takes away the trust which makes us want to share with others. Disgust takes away the good feelings and joy of living. Distance takes away closeness. Discounting and Disrespect come along to crumble up any IALAC that's left.

Everyone knows that the symbol for taking away is —.

 Some people are so good at taking away they don't even

know that the Dis family are their enemies, and can ruin their IALAC's and others too.

But once there was a man on earth named Jesus who understood about IALAC's and the Dis family. He saw Distrust and Disgust everywhere and He felt Distance especially. So one day He put His whole life into the battle against these enemies. His arms were stretched out to all people and a wonderful thing happened. The minus sign, −, became a + which we call the cross! Whenever we see a cross it can remind us that the Dis family was conquered. Instead of taking away we can put back trust, respect, closeness, and joy because of Jesus.

Here are some things to remember about IALAC's:

1. They must be cared for everyday.
2. If one gets torn up it's an emergency just as serious as a broken arm or fractured skull.
3. Immediate first aid is needed. By being present, listening, and understanding IALAC's can be miraculously mended.
4. Appreciation and encouragement are like vitamins for keeping IALAC's healthy.
5. Criticism and judgment are poison to IALAC's.
6. Forgiveness is like a heart transplant and can bring life back to IALAC's.
7. God has entrusted us with our own IALAC and with other's too. He wants to help us learn how to be good keepers of IALAC's.

Esther Howard is the mother of four grown children. She lives in Columbia, Maryland, where she conducts Family Enabling Groups.

A RHYTHM STORY: THE PRODIGAL SON

There once was a man
Who had two sons.

And one fine day
The younger one came to his father and said,
"You got some bread that is saved for me?"
"Yes, I got some bread that is saved for you."
"I'd like to have it now."
"Sure thing, son, no sooner said than done."

PAUSE

On the next day,
Early in the morning,
Jack got on the road and took on off.
With a breeze on his back and the sun shining down,
He was so happy
He could sing a song:
"I'm freeee,
I'm freeeeee,
I'm freeeeeee,"
Or so he thought.

PAUSE

When he got to the city,
He was spending the bread
Like it's going outa' style:
Wine—, women and song,
Alligator shoes, fine silk suits,
And a real fine pad.
With color TV's,
A big round bed
With mirrors on the ceiling.
Oh, he loved himself!
150 Or, so he thought.

PAUSE

But it didn't take long.
He had blown *all* the bread
Not one thin dime
To pay the rent
Or to buy some food,
And no more friends.
He needed a job but couldn't find one.
So he ended up
With a *lousy* job!
What a stinkin' job!
Just feeding some pigs.
Whatever was left that the pigs didn't eat,
Became *his* supper.
Humiliation!

PAUSE

Then one fine day he said to himself:
This is really *stupid*.
I'm going back home, and I'll say to my dad:
"If you take me back
I'll be your servant."
Or so he thought.
So Jack got on the road and started on home.
When he got pretty near,
His father rushed out with a hug and a kiss
To welcome him back.
Jack tried to talk about being his servant.
But his father said to him:
"Nooooo way!"
"Here's some alligator shoes
And a new silk suit.

151

We'll barbecue a cow
For a real big party.
My son has returned
Hoo . . . rayyy"

PAUSE

Meanwhile,
Out in the fields aworking away
Was the older son.
And he heard all the noise
Of a real swingin' party
So he came to the house to see what was happenin'
And he said to his father
"What's going on?
I'm working like mad.
The young punk returns from his whoring around.
You give *Him* a party."
So he got himself a sign
And *picketed* the party:
He got a bad deal
Or so he thought.
But his father said:
"Haaaay son!
You are *al*ways here
What's mine is *al*ways yours.
But your brother was dead!
Your brother was lost!
Now *he's* alive!
Now *he's* found!

AMEN!

A free adaptation from Luke 15:11–32
Gordon L. Nyenhuis

EPILOGUE

We said in the beginning that this book was still being written, and so it is. Our sincere hope is that you will write the next chapter—in your own patchwork family. We believe that you can do it, and with God's guidance you will. You have just read the beginning. The next step is yours. Good luck and good growth!

RESOURCES

In our work we have reviewed and used a number of resources. We have also learned of others involved across the US and in Australia who are working in this area. These resources are listed for your information.

INTERGENERATIONAL RESOURCES

1. *The Family Together, Intergenerational Education in the Church School* by Rogers and Rogers, Los Angeles: Acton House, Los Angeles, Calif., 1976
2. *Celebrating Togetherness* by Larson, Evangelical Covenant Church, Chicago, Ill., 1973
3. *Celebrate Summer* by McMahon and Huck, New York: Paulist Press, 1973
4. *Intergenerational Experiences in Church Education, JED*, Philadelphia: Geneva Press, 1976
5. *Generations Learning Together* by Griggs and Griggs, Griggs Educational Service, Livermore, Calif., 1976
6. *Family Cluster Resources*, Chicago, Ill.: Evangelical Covenant Church, 1977
7. *Mushroom Family*, published nine times a year: to subscribe write to F. C. Doscher, Box 12572, Pittsburg, Pa. 15241.

SMALL-GROUP PROCESS

1. *Serendipity Series* by Lyman Coleman, available through Word Books, Waco, Texas, through Serendipity House, Scottdale, Pa., and through religious book stores

2. *Values Clarification* by Simon, Howe, and Kirschenbaum, New York: Hart Publishing, 1972

3. *Teaching Your Child Right from Wrong* by Simon and Olds, New York: Simon and Schuster, 1976

4. *Meeting Yourself Halfway* by Simon, Niles, Ill.: Argus Communications, 1974

5. *Forty Ways to Teach in Groups* by Leypoldt, Valley Forge, Pa.: Judson Press, 1967

6. *Values Clarification as Learning Process, A Sourcebook* by Hall, New York: Paulist Press, 1973

7. *Christian Educators* by Hall and Smith, New York: Paulist Press, 1973

8. *Experiential Education* by Hendrix, Nashville: Abingdon, 1975

9. *Ideas*, published periodically by Youth Specialties, San Diego

10. *Creative Love* by Evans, Old Tappan, N. J.: Revell, 1977

11. *Happiness Is a Family Walk with God* by Bock and Working, Old Tappan, N. J.: Revell, 1977

12. *Happiness Is a Family Time Together* by Bock and Working, Old Tappan, N. J.: Revell, 1975

13. "Family Time, A Revolutionary Old Idea," Booklet #5000, by Nutt, c/o Family Time, PO Box 1000, Des Plaines, Ill. 60018

14. *Reaching Out* by D. Johnson, Englewood Cliffs, N. J. Prentice-Hall, 1972.

IDEAS FOR DISCUSSION AND WORSHIP

1. *Recycle* by Benson, a monthly periodical sharing

ideas from around the country: to subscribe write *Recycle*, Box 12811, Pittsburg, Pa. 15241

2. *Faith at Work* Magazine, edited by W. Howard, published eight times a year, contains special section in each issue on group activities; write Word Inc., 4800 West Waco Drive, Waco, Texas.

3. *JED SHARE*, a quarterly exchange of Christian education ideas, programs, resources, and concerns: to subscribe, write to *JED SHARE*, 1505 Race Street, Philadelphia, Pa. 19102.

4. *Catch the New Wind* by Zdenek and Champion, Waco: Word Books, 1972

5. *Come to the Party* by Olsson, Waco: Word Books, 1972

6. *Find Yourself in the Bible* by Olsson, Minneapolis: Augsburg, 1974

7. *Life on the Patio* by Olsson, Minneapolis: Augsburg, 1977

8. *One Inch from the Fence* by Seeliger, Atlanta: Forum House, 1973

9. *With Open Hands* by Nouwen, Notre Dame, Ind.: Ava Maria Press, 1974

10. *Hope for the Flowers* by Paulus, New York: Paulist Press, 1972

11. *The Way of the Wolf* by Bell, New York: Seabury Press, 1970

12. *Parables of Peanuts* by Short, New York: Harper and Row, 1968

13. *You Can Choose Christmas* by Reid, Waco: Word Books, 1975

14. *Even a Worm* by Blandford, Cincinnati, Ohio: World Library Publications, 1973.

15. *The Heart of Paul* by Johnson, Waco, Texas: Word Books, 1976

OTHER PEOPLE

In addition to the authors previously listed, we have learned of individuals working in this area:

1. Bonnie Agar, First Presbyterian Church, Bethlehem, Pa.
2. Rev. Dick Waggener, Sunday School Board, Southern Baptist Convention, 127 Ninth Avenue North, Nashville, Tenn. 37234
3. Covenant Church, Redwood City, Calif.
4. Margaret Sawin, Ed.D., First Baptist Church, Rochester, N. Y.

AUSTRALIA

In May and June of 1977, David Scott from Australia toured the US, researching the field of intergenerational education and activities. He included in his trip report a list of people contacted and resources reviewed. Portions of his list are reproduced here with his generous permission. His address is: David Scott, 62 Central Avenue, South Australia, 5072

People:

1. Mrs. Cathy Quaas, 4055 Jurupa Ave., Riverside, Calif. 92506—has designed and led I/G choir, is trained in Family Cluster
2. Virginia Hughes, 38660 Lexington # 427, Fremont, Calif. 94536—wrote her dissertation on I/G learning, has an excellent list of I/G objectives which are worth seeing
3. Allan Pollock, First Baptist Church, 8th and Main, Corona, Calif. 91720—has written up two experiences of adapting the Family Cluster model to an I/G Christian Education program
4. William Dorman, Westchester Christian Church,

8740 La Tijera, Los Angeles, Calif. 90045—has designed and led some summer I/G experiences called "Summer Fun Time" and is experienced in Family Cluster

5. Mildred Arnold, 760 S. Westmoreland Ave., Suite 364-70, Los Angeles, Calif. 90005—director of the Metropolitan Learning Center and trainer of Family Cluster leadership as one of many skills

6. Dorothy Knox, 2026A W. Cactus Road, Phoenix, Ariz. 85029—curriculum writer for *Sunday School Plus*, materials which are excellent for I/G learning

7. Ralph and Mary Detreke, 1451 Dundee Ave., Elgin, Ill. 60120—co-directors of Family Life Ministries (called Life-cycle Ministries) for the Church of the Brethren, trainers of Family Cluster leadership

8. Norman Stolpe, 222 W. Adams Street, Suite 395, Chicago, Ill. 60606—writer for *Family Concern* which produces some excellent material for family ministries geared especially for singles, couples, and parents

9. Lyman Coleman, 6139 S. Windemere Street, Littleton, Colo. 80120—producer of the "Serendipity" materials which now include evenings for parents and which are most useful in I/G events

10. Virginia Haney, 302 N. Dunton, Arlington Heights, Ill. 60005—director of Christian education, First Presbyterian, Arlington Heights

11. Joe Leonard, Family Life Education, American Baptist Convention, Valley Forge, Pa. 19481—has produced a kit on I/G approaches and heads up this area for American Baptists

12. Don and Pat Griggs, 1731 Barcelona Street, Livermore, Calif. 94550—coauthors of the book, *Generations Learning Together*, plus other materials

13. John Hendrix, Baptist Sunday School Board, 127 Ninth Avenue North, Nashville, Tennessee 37234—heading up some I/G experiments for Southern Baptists,

coauthor of the book, *Experiential Education*

Others involved in I/G approaches but not contacted on the trip:

14. Wayne Rickerson, 13600 SW Allen Blvd., Beaverton, Ore. 97005
15. Richard Ziglar, 913 S. Boulder, Tulsa, Okla. 74119
16. Louise Waschow, 73 Montford Ave., Mill Valley, Calif. 94941
17. George Koehler, PO Box 840, Nashville, Tenn. 37202

Resources:

1. "Planning I/G Experiences," a folder of materials and reprints relating to using the Bible, an I/G Sunday School, workshops, extended-family ideas, and the *JED* booklet by Mary Ducket, "I/G Experiences in Church Education"

—Joe Leonard

2. "Experiential Exercises for Family Clusters," twenty-eight experiential exercises used within Family Clusters but very suitable for wider use in I/G work

—Louise Waschow

3. "Learning Together," a guide for I/G education in the church—an excellent resource which deals with the basic theory of I/G approaches, as well as giving program ideas and designs

—Dr. George Koehler

4. "Learning Together: Resources for I/G Study," a packet of program designs and reprints of articles related to I/G approaches, plus a listing of resource people

across the US, published by Graded Press, United Methodist Publishing House

5. *Church School Magazine*, a monthly journal for Christian educators which, among many good things, includes a regular section devoted to I/G approaches (Resources for Family Groups)—published by United Methodist Publishing House, 201 Eighth Avenue South, Nashville, Tenn. 37202